SEAN OF THE SOUTH
VOLUME I

SEAN DIETRICH

Copyright © 2015 Sean Dietrich

All rights reserved.

ISBN-13: 978-1515019183
ISBN-10: 1515019187

DEDICATION

This book is dedicated to Lyle and Sherry Sandquist, who are family to me. To Melissa Wheeler, and Lanier Motes, who are also like family to me. And to my wife, Jamie, who is my bridge toward sanity and creativity, and the reason our car insurance payments aren't late each month. For this, I am grateful.

ACKNOWLEDGMENTS

To all the people who read my writings every morning on Facebook, or my blog, thank you. It is because of your support and love that I'm even taking the time to compile these stories into book format. I'll be honest, words fail me. So I'll just say, thanks. And thank you once again.

BERRYDALE

Off Highway Eighty-Seven, just before the Alabama border, is a service station in Berrydale. If you've never been to Berrydale, you don't know what you're missing. It's a town of about four hundred residents. Most keep their fridges on the back porch, and burn their trash in an oil drum.

Good folks.

The service station is among the last of its kind. It doubles as an eatery, and it's a hot-spot for Berrydalians. The whole town goes there, and I can't blame them. They have a biscuit sandwich that tastes just like deep-fried cherubs singing Handel.

Whenever I pass by, I stop in for a sandwich. And the girl behind the counter never forgets my face. To her, I'm sweetie. She's at least a decade younger than me. When she sees me walk through the door, she rustles up a sandwich and some fried corn nuggets.

Corn nuggets are the best things before sliced bread.

A few days ago, I stopped by. There she was, loading my little Styrofoam box with a handful of something.

I could've asked her to marry me.

"I gave you something different today," she said. "It's free."

"Free? Why?"

"Because legally, I can't charge you for this kind of biscuit sandwich."

I opened up the foam box and looked inside.

She smiled her three teeth at me. "I just caught that bullfrog last night. Joker had legs like Michael Jordan."

I smiled back at her. "You forgot my corn nuggets."

THE MANAGER

It was late. I was somewhere between Milton and Crestview when I stopped at a Mexican restaurant. It was a rundown place, with two cars in the parking lot. My waitress was a Mexican sweetheart. A woman in her sixties, only twenty-six inches high. She looked tired, like she'd worked long hours – for years.

Somehow, she was cheerful.

The two loud men at the table behind me gave the waitress a hard time. They'd worked up a good beer-glow. You could've blindfolded them with a piece of yarn.

They didn't want to pay their bill. The waitress was having difficulty understanding their logic. And their English.

So was I.

"I ain't paying for this," the young man insisted. "I wanna talk to the manager."

"Como?" she said. "No entiendo."

"Your man-a-ger."

I had all I could stand. I walked over to the table and stood beside the munchkin waitress.

"I'm the manager here," I said.

The men exchanged looks. "You? You're the manager?"

"That's right. What seems to be the problem today?"

I've always wanted to say that.

They didn't answer me. They removed cash from their pockets, slammed it down, then left. I watched their car speed away through the window.

She thanked me, and I answered with a line from a John Wayne movie.

When I moseyed to my truck, she waved goodbye. And if I'd had a hat, I would've tipped it to her.

That's when I stumbled on the curb and busted my lip open.

EIGHT-FEET TALL

In the checkout line before me stood a boy. Not just a boy. A growing boy, he must've been eight feet tall, weighing in at a-buck-ten. Sopping wet. He was a tower. If he were to fall down he'd be halfway home.

One thing about growing boys: sometimes they need peanut butter. This, I know from experience. But they don't just want plain peanut butter. No. They want it encased in a thin layer of chocolate and wax-paper – with ridges on the sides.

You can't reign in cravings like that.

Reese's are a childhood pastime, ranking somewhere between puppies and the World Series. They are perfect treats, and cannot be improved upon.

The boy set the Reese's down on the checkout counter. Then he fumbled through his pockets and counted his loose change. He was as slow as an iron toad, wearing a concerned look on his face.

The cashier waited patient.

I stepped forward. "Hey Stilts, you got enough?"

He shook his head.

"I got it." I reached for my wallet. "How much is it?"

He shrugged. "With or without the Mountain Dew?"

"Mountain Dew?"

"I really want a Mountain Dew to wash the Reese's down."

It was a reasonable suggestion.

"Go get one," I said.

The boy jogged away while I waited. When he returned, he set down the soda, along with another package of Reese's.

"Two Reese's?" I said. "You must be super-hungry."

He grinned at me. "No, that one's for you."

BROTHER RAY

My only encounter with a celebrity happened in New Orleans. I was seventeen, and I'll never forget it. Ray Charles had been my idol since I was old enough to pee standing up.

It happened like this: a friend and I were driving through the downtown. We had no intentions of staying, we were only passing through. Bourbon Street terrified the Budweiser out of us. We were as babyish as green tomatoes back then. The wildest party we'd ever attended involved three girls, a pig, and a can of shaving cream.

We wouldn't have known what to do in the Quarter but gawk and eat popcorn shrimp.

I rolled my truck to a stoplight. Something gargantuan pulled up beside me. A tour bus.

"Hey look," said my friend. "Is that who I think it is?"

"It can't be." I rubbed my eyes.

It was.

Overcome with excitement, I did something foolish. I cranked my window down and waved to Ray Charles himself.

Without missing a beat, Ray lifted his sunglasses and waved back at me.

I nearly passed a kidney stone.

Ray leaned out the window and shouted, "Hey honkie, the light's green." Then he laughed, and the bus drove away.

You could've knocked me over with a cotton ball.

That was years ago, and I'm nothing like that seventeen year old anymore. God knows, they couldn't pay me enough to be that age again. But my friend still keeps in touch. He sends me a birthday card every year.

He addresses it to Honkie.

TRY IT NOW

I pulled over somewhere outside Mobile, into a grocery store parking lot. She was loading her screaming kids into the car. You could hear them three states away. When I walked past her, she wore a helpless look on her young face.

She didn't have the courage to ask for help.

So I asked her.

"Ma'am, is there something you need?"

She leaned against her door. "My car won't start."

Those words. I heard them a lot growing up. I wish I could tell you how many times my father helped a hapless soul with a busted vehicle. It was his gift to the world before he died. Working on engines.

He'd lean into the guts of a stranger's Chevy and call out, "Try it now!" And it would eventually start.

He'd make certain of it.

I told the woman to pop the hood.

I peered into her engine. Lucky for her it was the battery. I was hoping for something more challenging. Maybe a bad spark plug, or a distributor cap.

I grabbed the jumper cables. It fired right up. Then I helped her load groceries into the backseat. She tried to offer me a twenty-dollar-bill.

I swatted her away.

I could hear my daddy's voice. "I don't want your damn money. You'd do the same thing for me."

Folks would always reply, "Absolutely."

I smiled at her. "I don't want money. You'd do the same for me."

She laughed. "Hell no I wouldn't."

I saw how she loved those babies. She's a liar.

SADIE

Sadie is my niece. A furry piece of chocolate with an open-mouthed smile. She belongs to my wife's brother and sister-in-law.

She's a family fixture.

Let me rewind twelve years: I didn't know Jamie well. I was a stranger, trying to make a good impression on her parents. It wasn't easy. Her mother didn't say much. I had to repeat my sentences to her daddy.

This chocolate pup parked herself by my feet.

She knew how to make me feel welcome.

A few years later, family vacation: I was newly married, and I'd just lost my job. Not a great year. I thought the world was out to get me, I did a lot of feeling sorry for myself. She trotted beside me on beach walks. Clever Sadie knew better than to baby me.

Over the course of time, Jamie and I moved into a bigger house. I remember it like yesterday. For once in our young marriage, we could afford the internet. That same year, Sadie had a mess of puppies. The first photos we received by email were puppies.

Another year, after my back surgery: Sadie went on vacation with us again. I had to stay inside, I couldn't do much moving around. The old girl laid by my feet most of the trip.

She knows things.

I saw Sadie last week. She's old. Her face is dandelion-white, she limps more than she walks now. But she makes you feel welcome with that open smile of hers.

When you pet her, you smile the same way.

COKE

Peanuts in Coca-Cola. Fifteen years ago, I'd never heard of such a thing. Not ever. I credit Jim Martin, my father-in-law, for showing me how it was done.

The first time I saw him do it was at a Martin family reunion several years ago.

See, once in a blue moon, the Martins throw a herculean Baptist barbecue, with all the fixings. Potato salad, baked beans, and lots of tomato aspic.

Everything except beer.

Millions of family members attend, even a few elders dating back to Enoch Martin – the youngest son of Adam and Eve Martin. My wife's relatives all have similar names too. It can be confusing.

There's a Mary, a Katherine, and a Mary Catherine. A handful of Bens, fourteen Jims and Jameses, some Johns, a couple Roberts, and a John Robert. There's a Les and a Lester, a few Phillips, and thirty-seven women named Flossie.

But only one Blake.

My father-in-law pulled a Coca-Cola from the cooler,

then loaded it with salted peanuts and took a sip.

"Brother Jim," I asked. "What are you doing?"

He looked at his older sister Katherine. They both giggled at me.

"Ain't you never heard of peanuts in Coke, boy?"

I shook my head.

"Here, try mine." Jim handed me his Coke.

I took a swig.

I spit the Coke out of my mouth. "Gross!"

"What, you don't like it?" He grinned.

"Real mature, Brother Jim." I wiped my mouth and glared at him. "You spit your potato salad back into this Coke."

ROUND BALES

Yesterday, on the outskirts of Samson, Alabama, I found myself stuck behind a round baler. He traveled about eight miles per hour. He poked his hand out the window and waved me on. I ignored him. The weather was perfect, too beautiful to drive fast.

If you don't know what baling is, you don't know what you're missing. It's marvelous. You owe it to yourself to visit your nearest Hick-Town, USA, and watch the first cutting of a foraging crop. Chances are, you'll find it as interesting as watching a television test-signal in black and white.

Unless you grew up baling hay.

I can remember the first spring cuttings as a boy. The green smell in the air was strong enough to taste on our tongues. The sunburns were nasty, the work thankless, our shoulders weak. I wish we'd have known back then that it was fun labor.

Because we all stood in line to hate it.

The baler pulled over to the side of the road to let me pass.

I pulled up next to him and rolled my window down.

He was a young man of about eighteen years. His lower lip was stuffed full – the same way ours were at that age.

"What're you baling today?" I called out to him.

He gave me a funny look. "Fescue, and some orchard."

"Great day for it."

He shook his head from side to side. "Man I hate doing this."

"God, don't I know it." I said. "But one day, you'll miss it."

OYSTERS

"But, I'm not sure I'll like oysters," the man on the stool next to me whined.

"Sure you will hun," his wife answered. "They're delicious."

"They look disgusting."

"Hush."

"I want to go to Olive Garden."

She laughed. "I didn't come all the way to Florida to go to Olive Garden."

So he pouted like a seventh grade girl.

The man wore a pressed shirt, with a collar starched sharp enough to split an apple. His accent sounded exotic and foreign, like he was from Des Moines. I took a peek at his shoes, they cost more than my education did. And that's really saying something.

It took me eleven years to finish college.

The waitress slid a tray of a dozen oysters before me. Pressed-Shirt eyed my platter with a funny look on his face. I slurped one from its shell, careful to make the loudest, sloppiest sound I could.

He watched me and curled his lip.

I selected another big one, then licked the oyster like a golden retriever cleaning himself.

"Is that good?" he finally asked me.

"What? This?"

He nodded.

"They're not good." I held up a slimy one. "They're great."

Tony the tiger couldn't have said it better.

He leaned in and looked at the gray thing. "What do they taste like?"

I thought for a moment, back to what my father-in-law used to say about bivalves.

"Well," I said. "They taste like whale snot and Tabasco sauce."

They went to Olive Garden.

ETHEL

I'll call her Ethel, though that's not her real name. I met her in the Walmart checkout line. A little about her: Ethel's eighty-three years old, from Luverne, Alabama and wears a skimpy bikini.

One with flowers on it.

I helped her out to her car, then loaded the groceries into her Buick. I did my absolute best not to stare at her. I looked at the ground instead. It felt indecent to make eye contact with an elderly woman not wearing enough to fry chicken safely.

But that didn't mean she wasn't a sweetheart.

She was.

Ethel came to Florida to see her grandbabies roll around in the sand. It's only the second time she's been to our sunny state, even though she lives two hours away. She said she worked all her life and never had time to vacation.

By the looks of her hands, I'd say she was telling the truth.

Long ago, when first married, her husband promised

her a trip to Miami. He swore they'd drink fruity drinks right on the beach and stay in one of those motels with plastic flamingos out front.

But he never got around to retiring.

He died two years ago.

"See," Ethel explained. "The trouble with being poor is it takes up all your time."

I helped her crawl into her driver's seat with my eyes closed.

"I'm off," Ethel told me. "I'm 'bout to go on the beach and watch my grandbabies swim."

I hope someone makes that woman a fruity drink.

COMMERCIAL APPEAL

The living room was full of nephews and friends. Five testosterone-machines filled the den, splayed on couches. Together they discussed vital matters of boyhood. Things like: who would win a fistfight between Batman and Spiderman, which gun is optimal for combat situations, and which boy has, in truth, eaten the most macaroni and cheese in one sitting without messing himself. The award went to me on that one.

During the height of the repartee, the room fell silent. Each boy's attention became glued to the television. Their eyes, the size of silver dollars. I looked at the television. A buxom brunette, wearing a strand of dental floss, waltzed across the screen.

No boy said a word.

When the commercial was over, the den was as quiet as a sanctuary. Reverent. No one was able to utter a thing of Batman or mac and cheese.

"Boys," I said. "You can't pay attention to advertisements like that."

"What do you mean Uncle Sean?"

"I mean, real women don't look like that."

One boy pointed at the television. "She looked real."

The rest of the boys heartily agreed.

"Sorry," I said. "She's as fake as pro wrestling."

"Uncle Sean, fake girls need love too."

I smacked my forehead. "Real women have curves. Full hips, normal waists, and real hearts. For crying out loud, real girls eat pizza. Those half naked things are made of plastic."

"Hey!" my nephew exclaimed. "You're only saying that because Aunt Jamie is standing right behind you."

CIVIC LEAGUE COOKS

Yesterday, I made brownies for Memorial Day lunch. Not just any brownies, Mrs. Jean Scharnitzky's brownies. With buttermilk.

Yes. Buttermilk.

I got the recipe out of the Brewton Civic League Cookbook. I stole this hometown book from Jamie years ago. It's one of my most prized possessions.

I've used this little gem to prepare many a small-town-Alabama feast. Some of my greatest hits have included: Paula's Pickled Shrimp, Triple Orange Ambrosia, Coca-Cola Salad, Squirrel D'ete, Red Beans and Rabbit, and Miss Genie's Cracka-lackin' Cheese Biscuits.

You see, I don't know who these Brewton women are, but their recipes have been passed down to me in these pages. I'm a better person for it. Whenever I use this faded book, I think about the sweet ladies in simple bib aprons, with flour dusted hands, and beehive hairdos. I think about how they made biscuits, by memory. The way they fried chicken, by feel. How they whipped up batches of Mrs. Ruby Hagood's tea cakes, when unexpected company showed up.

And even though I'm not kin to some lady named Pauline – I don't even know her – when I eat her fudge pie, I might as well be her baby boy.

Call me sentimental, but cooking is affectionate. I can't think of a better way to send love across generations than with food.

CENTERFIELD

I saw him trying on ball gloves, he was the only boy in the aisle. He had a confused look on his face, wearing a mitt three sizes too small for his growing hand.It made me smile.

Picking out a glove is a big event in a boy's life. Monumental. Second only to choosing a puppy – or a girlfriend. I remember my leather mitts. I still have them. They're in good shape because I oiled them often as a child. They smell like axel grease and bacon to this day.

"Hey slugger," I said to the boy. "You need help?"

He shrugged. "Don't know what I'm looking for. I need a bat and a glove."

"Well, let's start with your position. What're you playing?"

"Centerfield."

"Easy, that's at least a twelve inch glove." I selected a nice one and handed it to him. "Try that on Willie Mays."

It was a perfect fit.

He inspected the price tag, then dug into his pocket. I

knew what he was doing. I've done the same thing myself.

Counting pennies.

"You don't want to skimp on your glove Old Timer," I cautioned. "It's worth the extra money."

He sighed. "I guess I can always use someone else's bat."

I winked at him. "Good call."

I waved goodbye. When I turned the corner, I plucked a big barreled baseball bat from the rack, and left it up front with the cashier.

It was only a twenty dollar bat.

But every boy needs his own thunderstick.

STUART

Stuart is eighty-six years young.

He's the oldest friend I have.

Stuart just bought a small red convertible for himself. Even though he already owns several Cadillacs. He crawled inside the car and smiled at me. He had to bend down low just to get in the seat. He told me he bought the car because he thought it'd look good on him.

It does.

Stuart gets his love of cars honest, his daddy ran moonshine back in Virginia. He told me his father was a rowdy old dog who zipped the backroads, always with a posse of lawmen on his tail. And, if ever the law wasn't behind him, it's because it was Sunday.

Of course, Stuart will tell you upfront, he's not a carman, but a pilot.

And by God he is.

He's had his head in the clouds since he was a teenager. I went flying with him a few times. Lord, he babied that Cesna 172. He spoke to it in a soft whisper, like it could hear him. He flew me over my own house. I looked out the window, Jamie stood in the yard waving a dishrag. I waved back. He pretended like he was going to dive-bomb her, and I cackled with delight.

Last year Stuart finally sold his Cesna. We all knew it killed him, though he'd never admit it. He won't ever fly again. He knows that. But he's not letting that stop him.

Because he can still fly a convertible.

THE WRITER

Writing. I was never very good at it.
I was too slow.
In third grade, Miss Williams told us to write an essay. The topic could be whatever we wanted. I wrote an articulate piece regarding Batman's struggle with mediocrity. It took me half the night. Miss Williams didn't find my argument convincing.
She gave me a D.
Fourth grade. Mrs. Everhardt assigned an essay about our favorite foods. I wrote a stunning soliloquy on the rise and fall of the modern biscuit. It was subtitled: Pilsbury Killed the American Housewife. It took a week to write. I got another D. She suggested I write with fewer commas.
But, that, was, so, hard, to, do.
Fifth grade. Mrs. Bruner despised me from the get go. She told us to write about pioneers in America. She was not impressed with my paper, Ernie Banks; Pioneer Short Stop Who Changed the World. I received an F. She told me I was fool-headed for writing about

baseball.

Fool-headed.

I'll never forget that word.

Then came sixth grade, that was my year. Mrs. Doerkson believed in me. She knew how to reach a slow student like me. I was the only student she assigned one hundred word compositions to. Every day. Weekends too. Whatever I wanted to write about. Even baseball. Then she'd correct my grammar and pin my stories to her wall. It wasn't schoolwork, it was her gift to me.

That sweet woman told me I was special.

And I half believed her.

WESTVILLE

Late afternoon. I stopped at the convenience store in Westville, Florida, located off Highway 10. Almost thirty miles from the Alabama state line. It's a nondescript building, with a pay phone out front and a cemetery across the street. Inside, three fellas lounged in lawn chairs, circled around a cooler.

One man offered me a beer.

I declined and told him I had somewhere to be.

"Where you got to be in such a hurry?" he asked.

Small town folks are nosy.

"Actually." I looked my watch. "I'm on my way home."

"Suit yourself." He nodded to the cooler. "But the beer is free."

He had a point.

I relented and sat down.

The old boys talked about everything that came to their minds. Including local gossip. They made me feel right at home. All of us laughed until we were purple. One older man cackled so hard he almost passed a kidney stone. No joke.

It was the most fun I've had in years.

In Westville, of all places.

When we were through laughing, the youngest man of the group wore a smile on his face.

"Y'all know I hated Westville," the kid said. "I know y'all remember how I tried moving up to Birmingham. Took a job laying carpet." He looked at me. "I couldn't wait to get away from here."

The men grew quiet.

"Hell," the kid said. "I was a fool. You can't find friends like this in Birmingham. You just can't."

The whole group raised their cans.

They knew what he meant.

FREEPORT HIGH SCHOOL

Freeport High School's graduation was last night. Jamie attended to support her students. And I attended to support Jamie. I wore khakis. So did almost every other male over the age of thirty. The ceremony was on the football field.Beside me sat an elderly woman, too old to be on her feet for long. She and I couldn't see anything from where we were in back.

"Did you hear that?" she asked. "They just announced my baby's name. Kyle."

"That's your baby?"

She grinned her three teeth at me. "That's him."

The truth was, she had lots of babies. She had five children, fourteen grandchildren, and a kitchen busier than Grand Central Station. She assured me she was proud of each baby. But Kyle was special. She couldn't hide it. Kyle was the first of the entire family to graduate high school.

Ever.

"None of us is smart," she explained. "I can't hardly read. So I did the best I could, I worked real hard. That's what dumb mommas do."

Only someone brilliant could make a comment that ridiculous.

"Kyle's going into the Army tomorrow." She pointed to her grandson. "He wants my banana pudding before he goes."

The lucky dog.

"Lord," she said. "That youngun loves food. But you'd never know it, look how skinny he is."

When the music played, I helped her clap for Kyle. She applauded with stiff brittle hands, then dabbed her eyes with a hankie. Kyle's face was the brightest in all Freeport.

Except for one old face in the back.

DONUTS

Let me tell you about donuts.

That's right. Big old glazed ones.

When we first got married, we lived a few skips away from Krispy Kreme. When the wind was right, I could spit off my balcony onto the roof of the place. It was marvelous.

We ate hot donuts whenever the mood hit us. Eleven days per week. Sometimes twelve. We'd begin and end our days with them.

Every occasion.

Whenever Jamie and I had an argument, we'd bury the hatchet over a dozen glazed. If we went out of town, a box was in the front seat with us. When we went to the beach; we had donuts. Dinner dates; donut-deserts. Bad days; consolation-donuts. Great days; reward-donuts. Even mediocre days, holidays, and rainy days. I ate so many, they called me Amazing Glaze at the drive-thru window.

It was a nice time to be alive.

But that was thirteen years ago, we're not like that

anymore. We eat healthier now. Lots of kale and nutritional yeast. Sometimes Jamie eats a Milk Dud or two, but that's as crazy as she gets nowadays.

Of course, that's not the only thing that's changed. We don't live in a tiny apartment anymore, or share a cellphone. We're not nearly as impulsive as we were back then, or as idealistic. We have a mortgage, insurance, and busy lives. We think about our cholesterol. We're adults now, same as everyone else. Donuts are for kids. We don't eat them much anymore.

But I like to remember when we did.

RUBBER CHICKENS

I saw him staring out at the bay. Mid-to-late-twenties. He had his knees drawn up into his chest, like he had a metric ton on his mind.

I opened the truck door, Ellie Mae bounded out. All legs. She lives to play in that bay. I tossed her rubber chicken far into the water, she swam out to it, scaring away every fish for miles.

"Pretty dog," he mumbled.

It was an understatement, but I let it slide.

"Don't tell her that," I told him. "Her head's big enough already."

Ellie Mae emerged from the water with the toy in her mouth. She dropped it on the shore next to him.

He looked at it.

"You'd better throw it for her," I advised. "She's liable to have a nervous breakdown."

He hurled it. Ellie tore out after it.

After a few more throws, the young man opened up to me. Turns out, he was from South Carolina. His fiancee had dumped him to marry his best friend. It made my stomach sting. It was a beach wedding. He wasn't invited, but drove down anyway. Showed up with a gift, but didn't stay for the ceremony. He traveled ten hours just to give the happy couple a food processor.

He almost worked himself up into tears.

Ellie dropped her rubber chicken at his feet again, then sat down. Dripping wet. She drilled her big eyes into him.

She didn't give a cuss about weddings or food processors.

Ellie Mae only cared about that toy.

SUMMER VACATIONS

Summer. My family didn't take vacations, my parents worked too much for that. But my mother made up for it with tomatoes. While many of my friends visited the Grand Canyon, or the beach, we ate Heirlooms

By the barrel.

That's because Mother had a productive garden. She tended it with bare hands, pulling weeds for hours in the sun. By June, we could see the Blackfoot Indian in her – she tanned better than anyone in the county. Daddy teased her about it, but only because he was jealous.

He sunburned faster than redheaded bacon.

Mother passed her entire summer behind a chicken wire fence, with her tomatoes. Beefsteaks, San Marzanos, and Purple Cherokees. She did more with that little plot of dirt than some people do with a Harvard degree.

That was her vacation.

One summer, my best friend went to Disney World. He was gone for two whole weeks, though it seemed like six years. He sent me a postcard of himself shaking

Mickey Mouse's hand.

It about killed me.

Mother glanced at the postcard. "Just look at that, some poor fool dressed up like Mickey Mouse to pay the bills." She winked. "I wouldn't shake hands with a rat. Filthy old things."

Mother walked over to the basket of Brandywine tomatoes on the washing machine. She rifled through them and selected the prettiest one. Then she sacrificed it on the cutting board. She fixed a ten-inch-high tomato sandwich that made Disney World look like a joke.

And then she split it with me.

ROY

His name was Roy.

He was hard at work trimming an overgrown bush at the end of our road. Courtesy of Walton County. He's been doing this-n'-that work for the county since Lyndon Johnson was in office. Old Roy's retired twice during his career, but it never took. He keeps ending up on government payroll again, installing speed bumps, replacing road signs.

He looked like he'd seen his share of Decembers.

"County work ain't what I really do." Roy showed me his fingertips. "I'm a guitar picker. It's how God made me."

His callouses were thick as boot leather.

Roy told me he wanted to be a famous singing cowboy once. He did what many young musicians did, he trucked up to Nashville. He didn't have enough silver in his pocket to operate a pay phone. "I wasn't above sleeping outside on a church lawn," he said. "God took care of me."

When he got to Music City, things looked good for

Roy. He played in a few legendary joints, even shared the stage with a few Nashville heavyweights. Though he wouldn't tell me who.

He said boasting was a sin.

But Roy's time in Opryland was short lived.

"I left," he explained. "I high-tailed it the moment I realized I weren't nothing special. Hell, I'm just a guitar picker from Freeport, Florida. I wanted to go hunting with my boys, kiss my wife. I'm an old redneck. Shoot, look at me. I ain't nothing remarkable."

I looked at him.

He seemed pretty damn remarkable to me.

INDEX CARDS

As a thirteen-year-old, it was apparent that I liked to cook. Though I was terrible at it. I'll never forget my first dish. Potato salad. I accidentally used sugar instead of salt. It tasted so bad the houseflies all pitched in to get our screen door fixed.

After my potato salad disaster, Mother had all she could stand. That Christmas she gave me a cookbook. Betty Crocker's Picture Cookbook. It once belonged to my grandmother. The thing was an antique, published in 1950. In the back of the book was a slew of index cards covered in frilly handwriting. My grandmother's writing. I learned how to cook with those recipe cards. I made everything from her oyster dressing to baked Alaska.

Though, I've only made baked Alaska once.

I promised the fire marshal I'd never attempt it again.

Yesterday, I found the cookbook in the attic, buried in an old box. Just seeing it catapulted me back twenty years. I remembered the Christmas I got it, and I thought about a grandmother I never knew.

I blew the dust off the book.

There was a card inside.

"Merry Christmas," Mother's handwriting read. "It's time you had your own cookbook, and this one's special. It belonged to my very best friend in the whole world. Now I'm passing it on to you. Mom would've wanted you to have it. I wish you could've known her, she made the best potato salad in the entire city."

My mother wasn't exaggerating.

I've made that potato salad a million times.

NO NEED FOR ALARM

Last night around ten o'clock, South Walton county's Walmart was the place to be. I counted five firetrucks, two ambulances, one disgruntled staff, and about sixty onlookers. A slew of rubberneckers held phone-cameras high, hoping for a glimpse of something awful. Something Facebook-worthy.

I was one such rubbernecker.

I approached a woman in a Walmart vest and asked her about the ordeal.

"Don't know," she said, taking a drag from a cigarette. "All I know is that fire alarm was loud. I thought it was a bomb."

A bomb. In Walmart.

As I live and breathe.

To be fair, I can see how an embittered shopper might be inclined to pull a prank on Walmart. There are certain scenarios that incubate this type of thing.

One such scenario happened to me recently. The store was filled to max-capacity with Florida tourists. Management shut down all checkout lanes, except the express lane, manned by Edna – a sweet old lady with hearing aids. The line backed up all the way to I-10. It got so bad, a frazzled man in line cracked open a beer.

Such rudeness among tourists is staggering.

He didn't even ask if anyone else wanted one.

After a long wait in the parking lot, they opened Walmart again. The fireman told us someone pulled the alarm. He told us it cost the county a shipload of money too. All because some clown thought it'd be funny to pull a prank.

Well, it wasn't funny.

I regret ever laying a finger on that stupid fire alarm.

WAR EAGLE

I stopped at a barbecue joint outside Salem, Alabama. A middle-aged man sat on the stool next to me. My first impression was that something was wrong with him. He made little grunts while he chewed his food.

The man turned and stared at me. Then he dug a notepad from his pocket and scribbled something down.

"Where are you from?" it read.

So I told him.

He bellowed a laugh, then flicked his ears. "I'm deaf," he said, butchering the words.

He handed me the pencil.

"I'm from Florida," I wrote.

He nodded. "I'm from Auburn." Then he moaned, "War eagle."

The waitresses giggled, and so did I.

He wrote again. "You look just like my son."

"Poor fella," I said. "He must have to swat the girls away with a stick."

The man let out one of those awkward laughs again. He removed his wallet and showed me a photo. Then he flashed it to the waitresses. They smiled like they'd seen it a hundred times already. In the picture stood a young man holding a baby girl. He didn't look a thing like me.

Not even close.

The man scrawled onto his pad. "Car accident. He's been gone a few years."

I didn't know what to say.

The waitress brought my check and set it on the counter. Before I could reach it, the man snatched it up and winked at me. That old joker was going to pay my bill whether I liked it or not.

He wasn't doing it for me.

A MAN'S BELT

"If you want to understand a man, pay attention to his belt," my grandfather once told me. "You'll learn a lot about him."

It struck me as an odd statement. I was only a boy at the time.

"Looky here," he grabbed his belt. "This stays with a man through everything. Forget his shoes, look at his belt."

He patted his buckle. "Got this in 1926. Picked it up in town, after my daddy died. I bought it five sizes too big. I wanted to be sure I had plenty to grow into, and I only wanted to spend my money once."

He laughed. "I punched holes in it to make it fit."

I looked at the old leather.

He told me he wore that simple thing nearly every day of his adult life. He wore it to school, or with a pair of slacks to church. He wore it to bail hay – the old fashioned way. He wore it to play baseball.

He had it on when he sang over the radio, and when he first danced with my grandmother.

He wore it to his wedding.

The belt was snug around his waist when he enlisted. It was with him in Europe, and when they awarded him a Purple Heart. When he gave my mother piggyback rides, and when he changed the oil in his Studebaker. He even wore it to his wife's funeral.

And when he and his redheaded grandson sat on lawn chairs, eating sunflower seeds by the fistful.

He had it on then too.

MY LEFT TOE

I waited in the vinyl chair, with sweaty palms. It was my big toe, the doctor thought it was infected. I hate hospitals. I would've rather been somewhere else than in that cheap chair.

The old man next to me fiddled with his fingernail clippers, he couldn't seem to jimmy them open. I offered my assistance.

He thanked me, then asked, "What are you in for?"

"My toe." I said. "It's infected."

"You seem nervous."

I nodded. "I really hate hospitals."

He thought for a moment. "You know I hurt my big toe once. It was bad. Happened while cleaning leaves in my gutter. Up on the roof. I tripped over our damn cat."

I laughed. "I don't get it, how did that break your toe?"

"My wife heard me hollering, I was stuck. My trousers snagged on the gutter. Couldn't move. Hell, I finally ripped my pants, I fell off the roof, landed on this foot." He pointed to his shoe. "That's how I broke it."

My laugh matured into a cackle.

Then, the nurse called my name.

I stood up and bid goodbye to my new pal.

"I see you made friends," the nurse whispered. "He's sweet. It breaks my heart. He used to sit here with his wife while she took treatments. Since she died, he still comes and sits, same exact place. For no reason at all."

I looked back at him, reading a magazine.

She was dead-wrong. He had a reason for being there.

That day, it was me.

WHAT ARE WE PLAYING?

My nephews and their friends played cards, on the sidewalk. I could tell by the way they fussed at each other they were playing Five Card Draw.

That's how we entertained ourselves as kids. Poker. We would've watched television, but our consoles only picked up two channels. One of which was PBS.

Nobody gave a cuss about PBS and its puppets.

Playing poker teaches you a lot about your friends. Some of mine were bad about paying up debts. My buddy Zip still owes me nearly seven hundred thousand dollars.

That's why he ignores me on Facebook.

"What are we playing boys?" I butted in.

"Five Card Draw."

I scoffed. "No, no. This is all wrong. You can't play Five Card, you're nearly grown men."

"So?"

"So, grown men play Texas Hold'em."

They stared at me like I was purple.

Thus, I taught them the best game in America. I

explained the flop, the turn, and the importance of owning a good pair of sunglasses. They were mesmerized. After a few educational rounds, we got down to business.

Uncle Sean won four dollars.

We played again.

I won four more.

We tried another hand.

I won a dollar, and three extra-small T-shirts.

After the fifth win, Uncle Sean used his smartphone to book a room in Biloxi.

Then along came the neighbor-boy's little sister. She was missing her front teeth. I persuaded the boys to let her play a hand – to be nice. Everybody wants to feel included.

And now she owns my truck.

SUSAN

My friend Susan just got married. I haven't seen her since I was knee-high to a Coke bottle. She's in her mid-thirties now. I still remember her when she was a gangly girl who complained about her long face and knobby knees. Though I never noticed any of that.

She was my friend.

My mother instructed me not to treat Susan like just any old pal. Susan was a lady. Mother said it was up to gentleman-boys to compliment ladies – it's a duty.

"Compliment her hair," Mother suggested. "Or her shoes."

"But she wears ugly pink shoes."

"It doesn't have to be her shoes, pick anything. Girls need compliments."

Fair enough.

The next day, I put Mother's advice into practice. I told Susan she had lovely eyes. Her face got red. She suggested I substitute poison ivy for toilet paper. Then she horsewhipped me with a tetherball.

I tried to heed Mother's words. I complimented Susan

on everything from the tassels of her bicycle handlebars, to her impressive sticker collection. And for each adulation, Susan would award me with a swift fist to the stomach.

That's what ladies do.

I remember the day Susan learned her parents were getting divorced. Neither of us knew what that word meant, but we knew it was bad. I put my arm around her and pulled her tight against me. Susan buried her head in my shoulder and moaned.

I couldn't think of a single comforting thing to say.

So I told her I liked her pink shoes.

COWBOYS

I almost saw a Willie Nelson concert when I was twelve. It would've been my first concert. Ever. Willie was a lot younger then, and had a worse voice than he does now. KXRP announced it on the radio every few minutes.

"Come see Willie in August," the announcer would blare. "Live at the arena, singing the hits we know by heart."

Oh I knew them by heart alright.

And I planned to sing some duets with old Willie.

It took me most of the summer to save up enough. I found a job cleaning out my neighbor's horse stalls every morning. It was easy work. They paid me nine bucks a week to shovel whookie and clean tack. By the end of July, I'd saved enough. I called the radio hotline, sent in my cash, and received my ticket in the mail.

But, it wasn't meant to be.

On the day of the concert, I came down with a one hundred and two degree fever. Mother said I was so hot my brains were about to boil into a pot of collards.

Daddy had to look after me while Mother worked the night shift.

And so it was, while Willie crooned to his fans, Daddy force-fed me Jell-O in bed. He stayed at my side all night. I remember he sang softly, "Mamas don't let your babies grow up to be cowboys." He sang it with his eyes closed.

He knew every single word.

And his shaky voice put Willie's to shame.

TALL TALES

My daddy loved to tell the story about the huge scar he had. He got it carrying a bottle-flask of whiskey in his back pocket as a teenager. He fell backward on the pavement and the glass shattered. His hindparts were never the same.

My pals would roll on the floor laughing at that story.

He told good ones. He embellished the hell out of them, too. I'm certain his tales were seventy percent horse apples.

Maybe eighty.

One of his classics: the time he sassed his mother. Daddy tore out the screen door before she could swat him. He zipped through the pasture, hopping fences. After a mile or so, he decided he was safe. When he turned to look behind him, she was hurdling fences like a thoroughbred.

She strung him up by his tongue and shaved his head.

Another tale he told: about the time he fell off a building. A true story. He fell while welding, three stories, smack-dab onto his head. They thought the fall paralyzed him, somehow it didn't. He always finished with the same punchline. "Doctors X-rayed my head, but they never found nothing."

He had anecdotes for all occasions.

I remember when he found me crying on the porch. I didn't make the baseball team. He sat beside me and said, "The bad things that happen in life, are great stories in disguise. If you pay attention, you'll find some good tales to tell."

He passed shortly thereafter.

This is one of those tales.

FAKEBOOK

I first logged on Facebook in 2009. Social media was a new concept. I could see what all six of my friends had to say about themselves. Usually, only a sentence or two.

I remember posting: Hello world, it's Tuesday.

I'm not sure why.

Before long, my entire hometown was online. I accrued two hundred Facebook friends overnight. I kept current on everyone's lives without having to wear pants.

Right on my computer.

It was great.

Like when Uncle Pete bought a bulldog better-looking than he was. Or when Aunt Edna got hacked. Obscene photos popped up on her wall, and we all assumed she was the one in the pictures. Two hundred comments later; the whole town banded together to buy her a better camera.

After a few years, Facebook changed. My newsfeed deteriorated into mush. Teenage selfies, superhero hamsters, and some rotund fella in a Speedo, dancing aerobics. Then there's those multiple-choice tests to see which Disney Princess you most resemble.

I got Cinderella's stepsister.

Some viral tidbits are ridiculous. Take for instance: the video of my second cousin twerking along to the National Anthem. Three million views. It left me speechless – with my hand over my heart.

That boy ain't never been right.

How about the quiz to discover your ideal soulmate? I was excited about that one. After a forty-five minute test, they told me to try Craigslist. And don't forget all the inappropriate pics my sweet aunt Edna posts. She has over ten thousand followers now.

We should've never bought her that camera.

TUESDAYS

Tuesdays are fried catfish night in DeFuniak Springs, Florida. Whole catfish. Tails and all. Maclain's buffet has everything. Mediocre hushpuppies, an iceberg lettuce bar, and tattooed waitresses who can lift Buicks over their heads.

I ate so much catfish I forgot my wife's name.

Through the front door walked a herd of Mexican boys, wearing filthy clothes. They looked like they'd earned their suppers. Each piled his plate high. One boy balanced two plates, a soda, and a bowl of ice cream.

A little later, a crew of loud teenagers walked in. Boys of privilege, with new trucks, clean boots, and camouflage ball caps.

And girlfriends.

The tableful of Latinos noticed the brunettes in hot pants. And while the girls didn't mind the attention, their boyfriends did. One of the boyfriends – let's call him Bo Duke – didn't care for the way Don Juan gawked at Daisy.

Bo glared at the Mexican boy.

"What're you lookin' at moron?" Bo confronted.

Don Juan didn't answer.

Bo laughed. "'S'what I thunk."

Bo's sidekicks snickered, they appreciated his no-nonsense command of the English language. The Mexican boys gave no response. They kept their heads down and finished their meals in silence.

And then they left.

After I paid our bill, Jamie and I walked outside. We were both sick from eating too much catfish. I had to loosen my belt so that I could breathe without getting all sweaty.

Then, I noticed something unusual in the parking lot.

Three shiny monster trucks, sitting pretty.

With tires as flat as pancakes.

HENRY

My great uncle, Henry, used to give me coins whenever I saw him. It was his tradition. He gave silver dollars, buffalo nickles, and gold pieces, too. I don't know how much money he doled out over the years, I'm sure it was in the millions.

Once, he stayed at our house, visiting the area on business. Lord, I was rich. Every morning that joker had a coin for me. He'd plop it into my palm and I'd marvel.

I didn't care what it was worth.

Uncle Henry grew up rural, no stranger to hard work. And he had hands as big as skillets. I remember a tattoo on his forearm too, it was from the Navy. That's where he learned to play the guitar.

And God, could he pick.

Henry was white-hot on the steel string.

He never married. He rented a garage apartment from a widow named Sylvia. They ate dinner together and went to church arm in arm. They were a regular couple, for their entire adulthood. No one knows why they didn't marry. Years later, after she passed, he admitted he never slept in that dank apartment. Not a single night.

Sylvia would've beat him silly for saying such.

He died from pneumonia. It was a small funeral. Not many folks came. He had no children, and no in-laws. But I was there, so was Jamie. I walked up to the front of the church to say goodbye to him.

I counted thirty-three different coins sprinkled in his casket.

Counting mine.

LOCAL TOMATOES

"We got lucky," the woman said. "Finally, we got some damn rain. Our field peas were nearly dead from all this dry weather."

She lived in Dixonville, Alabama, a few feet over the state line. It's a community no bigger than a Persian rug. The woman sold vegetables from her front porch. Though she didn't have much of a porch – or a home for that matter. Her front yard was a dilapidated heap of rusted junk and a horse pen. Behind the dogtrot house was nothing but sprawling acres of vegetables.

The woman had mountains of tomatoes.

My daddy used to say I ate tomatoes like a bare-assed baboon ate plums. I never knew what that meant, but I had a feeling it was true. I love tomatoes.

"Sure is hot," Jamie said, loading a baggy full of produce.

"You can say that again," the woman answered. "After living here all my life you'd think I could tolerate the heat, but I can't."

Jamie filled a plastic bag with six pounds until it

threatened to spill. As many red beauties as the flimsy thing could hold.

"Let's see." The woman slid her glasses on and calculated the weight. "One dollar a pound. That'll be six dollars, ma'am."

Jamie shook her head. "No ma'am, it won't." Then Jamie dug into her pocket and slapped down a fifty-dollar-bill. "These tomatoes are worth at least fifty dollars, and you know it."

The woman flashed a tobacco-stained smile at us.

And I realized then, Jamie had stolen my wallet.

HE WAS OURS

"Hank used to practice guitar underneath this house," the old woman told me. "That's because it's cool down there, during the summer."

The old woman's name was Margaret. She gave me a tour of Hank Williams' boyhood home, located in the sleepy town of Georgianna, Alabama. She and I were the only two souls in that quiet clapboard house. The tour was five dollars, but I suspected she was giving me the five-hundred-dollar tour.

Since I was Tuesday's only visitor.

Miss Margaret is eighty-eight years old, and she's sweet as syrup. A stroke has paralyzed half of her face, but her brain works faster than mine. She's lived in Georgianna since 1951. She and her friend run the Hank Williams place, which is open six days a week. They've given the same five-dollar tours to George Jones, Loretta Lynn, Merel Haggard, Willie Nelson, Waylon Jennings.

And me.

She showed me everything there was to see. Where Hank practiced guitar, his favorite climbing trees, and where he'd shoot squirrels.

"The thing about Hank," she explained. "He sang for you and me. He played music for real folks. We were regular-hard-working-folks, and he was one of us."

She smiled a crooked smile. "It was more than just music. It was my generation. Those are the songs of our youth. It's what we danced to. Hank was ours. He was Alabama." She shook her head. "Music just ain't homemade like that today, and I don't think it'll be quite like that ever again."

No ma'am.

I don't believe it will.

GREG

Gardner Elementary School, I had a buddy named Greg. He was a strange fourth-grader. He had daily routines he lived by. Old Greg was the only boy in the entire school who carried a day-planner.

Odd.

Greg was an only child, but he wasn't spoiled. His parents divorced, his mother lived in Nevada, and his daddy worked two jobs. My mother told me that Greg was a latchkey kid.

I didn't know what that was.

What I did know was that Greg walked to school, unlike me. I rode the school bus. Each morning, Greg arrived to class before anyone else. Same time, every morning.

Greg liked to play the same game each recess too. So, for nine months straight we played foursquare. He also ate the same lunches. Campbell's soup and a cheese sandwich.

Same exact thing, every day.

Strangest fourth-grader in the county.

One weekend, several boys had a sleepover at Greg's place. His daddy worked the late shift, so we boys had Greg's empty house to ourselves. Greg prepared macaroni and cheese for supper. I brought Paydays and MAD magazines for dessert.

Afterward, we helped him do housework. I vacuumed the living room; Greg washed the dishes. Later, we all watched movies we weren't supposed to watch, while Greg folded the clean laundry.

His daddy finally rolled in around midnight. Greg's face lit up. He went to the kitchen and fixed his daddy the biggest sandwich we'd ever seen.

Yes, Greg loved that daddy of his.

Whenever he was lucky enough to see him.

HUMBOLDT

Humboldt. It's a nothing town. Tiny. Less than two-thousand people, and more farmland than you can shake a sickle at. The city's population drops by twenty families every year. Folks keep moving away. Maybe because there's nothing to do in Humboldt but bale hay or drink.

Or both.

The farmhouse where my daddy was born is a clapboard shack. It sits on eight miles of table-flat prairie. The inside of the house smells like dust and old sweat, and I suspect it always has.

In Humboldt, baseball is still a religion. At Humboldt High School, you can watch skinny rural boys play the game their great great grandaddies invented. They play on the same dirt that Sharky Sweatt and Big-Train Johnson once played on.

The same field where my daddy played catcher.

On the west side of town is the Neosho River, where I first learned to gut a fish. There, I discovered filet knives slice ten-year-old hands the same way they do trout. Down the road from there, is the Neosho Memorial Hospital. That's where they stitch up ten-year-old fishermen.

My daddy liked to visit Humboldt, any chance he got. Summers, we practically lived there.

I couldn't understand why he loved it, but he did. The closer we'd get to town the easier he breathed. As soon as we'd hit Highway 54, he'd drop thirty years. By Highway 169, he'd have a beer popped open, with his left arm hanging out the window. The miles of open pasture did that to him. Why the hell not, it's where he was born.

And it's only a stone's throw from where he died.

COOKING UP TROUBLE

As a young man, I worked as a cook for Waffle House. It was an easy job, except for all the work. There, I learned to clean a flat top, to fry eggs, and to wear a paper wedge hat. We called that hat the Confidence Killer. If you want to know why, go serve breakfast to the girl's varsity volleyball team at two in the morning wearing one.

You'll see.

One night, there were only two of us manning the store. Me and Harmony, a young waitress with a thick Southern accent. Three rowdy fellas came through the door. They'd been drinking. They talked loud and laughed at their own jokes a little too hard. Things got worse when one decided to put the moves on Harmony.

"Hey pumpkin," he said. "I have a library card, do you mind if I check you out?"

Harmony ignored him, but the fella was relentless. He stood up and put his arms around her. She struggled against him, but he wouldn't let up. She screamed.

That was when my blood turned to boiling syrup.

I don't know what came over me. I grabbed a carton of eggs and began throwing four-seamer fast-balls at him. The eggs splattered everywhere. To seal the deal, I emptied half a bottle of Tabasco sauce on the gentleman's scalp. Then, I sprayed him with a fire extinguisher until he resembled a snowman.

They finally left.

Later, while mopping up egg yolks, I learned the troublemaker was Harmony's husband.

If I'd known that, I would've used a lot more Tabasco.

HIGHWAY 127 YARD SALE

The Highway 127 Yard Sale is a seven-hundred-mile, junk-extravaganza. The event starts in Gadsden, Alabama, and hikes straight up the crotch of Godless Michigan.

Thirteen years ago my wife and I went, armed with a map and a clunky Oldsmobile. We stayed the first night near Mentone, Alabama. An old woman opened her farmhouse to yard-salers for ten bucks a night.

She had twenty-four cats and a donkey.

The following morning, I awoke to cats nestled in my armpits, and a donkey at the window.

Jamie and I were already starting to bicker. We squabbled through two hundred miles of antiques. That night, we collapsed at a motor-inn in Melvine that smelled like a pot of collards.

I found poop in my bed.

By the next day, Jamie was sick of my smug little face – she told me so. We argued all through Tennessee. Crosstown, Grimsley, Byrdstown, and finally settled in Albany, Kentucky. There, Jamie bought a fondue pot.

Thank God for that.

We needed one.

When we got to Union, Kentucky all hell broke loose. I got sideswiped by a transfer truck. It amputated my side-mirror. Our Oldsmobile resembled a tired Budweiser can. A few miles later, a tire blew out. No spare. We spent the night in the car with the windows open.

That night it rained.

Like holy hell.

Outside Cincinnati, Jamie threw my suitcase out the window. She locked me out and inched our car toward the Michigan state line without me. Finally, in Hudson, Michigan, our Oldsmobile transmission went to be with Jesus.

So did her fondue pot.

PECK OF PICKLES

I tried to make pickles last week. They came out tasting like cucumbers soaked in rubbing alcohol. I don't have the knack my mother had. She could've pickled boot leather and it would've been fit to serve company.

Pickling was her thing. Compared to hers, store-bought pickles were a joke.

Mother also claimed her pickle brine was a miracle elixir. Capable of relieving headaches and constipation. I never believed her claims until I was twelve. My insides were backed up worse than five-o'clock traffic. Mother made me drink an entire jar of pickle juice.

After forty minutes on my side, the Lord visited our house.

Mother pickled everything from hardboiled eggs to beef livers. Daddy loved slimy livers. I didn't want to be in the same county when he ate them. To be funny, he'd plop them on his face and pretend like they were gnawing him alive.

He made all the noises that might accompany such an event.

Mother's most famous pickled delicacy was watermelon rinds. In the summers she collected them. When she had enough rinds, she'd pickle them better than Peter Piper himself. But we were only permitted to eat them at barbecues.

When we had guests.

And not everyone appreciated watermelon rinds like we did. In fact, some didn't even know what they were. Once, my Uncle from New Jersey was visiting. Daddy barbecued a pork shoulder. When my uncle saw the rinds, he wrinkled his face like he was about to vomit.

He should've never done that.

Because then Daddy broke out the beef livers.

'79 CHEVETTES

I met Phillip in the parking lot. He was crawling into a 1979 Chevette. Red. My uncle had one just like it. I learned how to drive a stick in that thing.

Phillip must've been eighteen – he didn't look a day over eight. A clean shaven kid, skinny as my forearm. He was traveling east, across the Gulf Coast. Mississippi to Miami. He'd been living out of that Chevette of his.

Sleeping on the beach.

"I like sleeping on the beach," he told me. "They'll run you off some places, but most don't care. It's free air conditioning."

I asked Phillip why he was taking such a trip.

"Adventure." He shrugged. "My parents got divorced."

And he left it at that.

Phillip left Mississippi last month. Since then, he's been chasing summer adventure along Highway Route 98, on a budget. His little Chevette will run all day on a thimbleful of gasoline. In the backseat was assorted, cheap fishing gear. He told me he planned on catching his dinner each night to save money. So far, it wasn't working out. He hadn't caught a single fish.

Youth can be a potent hallucinogenic.

When Phillip tried to start his car, it wouldn't turn over. He popped the hood. It was evident this boy knew his way around that one-point-four-liter engine. After a few clicks with a ratchet, the Chevette fired right up.

Yes. I believe old Phillip and that Chevy will be just fine.

I just hope he finds that adventure.

God knows, they get harder and harder to come by.

JIMBO

"I started raising crickets in '97," said Jimbo. "Back when I's still a truck driver for Publix, in Jacksonville. Sold crickets on the weekends." He shrugged. "Just for fun."

Jimbo swatted a gnat from his face.

The Florida gnats were relentless. Judging by the amount of them on old Jimbo, he must've tasted better than I did.

A few years ago, Jimbo retired from his Publix job. His diabetes got out of control. "Shoot, no one wants to be told he's a liability," he said. "But my boss was right, I couldn't be on the road like this, not anymore."

Jimbo sold his semi truck and left Jacksonville. He moved in with his brother, a mortician outside Bristol, Florida.

"I spent a lot of time feeling sorry for myself," Jimbo admitted. "My brother offered me a job, but hell, funeral work ain't for me." He smacked a gnat on his cheek. "You got to be born for that kind of thing."

Figuring he had nothing to lose, Jimbo decided to sell

bait. Crickets and earthworms. He built a tiny plywood trailer with two air conditioning units. Then he stocked it with fishing paraphernalia and parked it along State Road 12.

He sold out of crickets his first day.

Nowadays business is steady, and Jimbo doesn't sit around pouting anymore. He hasn't any time to. He's too busy raising bait.

"Funny thing," Jimbo said. "Just when you think your life's over, you do something like open up a damn cricket stand."

Yes.

Funny things, those cricket stands.

KATHERINE

"I wanted to be a concert violinist," Miss Katherine said. "I've been playing since I was three."

Katherine Clark is ninety-one, but her Italian violin is much older. It dates back to Moses. It looks good for a relic, but not half as good as Katherine.

She got the violin when she was a young woman. A gift from a musical repairman who recognized her talent – and her brown eyes.

"A bus ran over it, destroyed it," Katherine explained. "The music store threw it away. The repairman dug it from the dumpster, put it back together, and he gave it to me."

Brown eyes make men do strange things.

At nineteen, Katherine packed her violin and traveled forty minutes east. "I taught school in Greensboro," she said. "It's tiny. The only things to do there were pick tobacco and go to church."

So she became a Baptist.

One Sunday, Katherine noticed a blue-eyed fella gawking at her during the sermon. The boy later introduced himself as Herschel. He was a tobacco farmer, and Katherine wasn't interested in farmers. She didn't want to be anything more than friends. And that's what they became. Such good friends, she ended up bearing four of his children.

She showed me a picture of Herschel on the wall.

"See, I wasn't supposed to be a famous violinist." Katherine smiled. "I make a better wife and mother."

She wedged the violin beneath her chin and played through a three octave scale. Up the neck and down again.

Just to prove she still could.

Well, she can.

BABY-DOLL

The elderly waitress called me baby-doll when she brought my plate of eggs. It made me smile.

I've always liked being called baby-doll.

But not by just anyone. I only like being called such names by older women. If pet names come from the wrong mouth, it's awkward. For instance: a few nights ago, our server kept calling me sugar-lickums. It didn't set well with me, but I still left a good tip.

At least the boy was trying.

The thing is, there are rules when it comes to pet name usage. You can't just throw names around. It's rude. I learned about some of these rules from my father-in-law.

"It goes like this," old Jim explained. "Boys are never permitted to use pet names, at any age. End of subject. It's disrespectful. And girls cannot use them until after high school. At that age, girls are free to use any nickname – provided the namee is younger."

"Namee?" I asked.

"The party receiving the nickname. See, if a waitress

calls a thirty-three-year-old man baby-doll, and she's twenty, it just ain't right. She can't use names on someone older."

I stopped him. "So girls can only use names on boys younger than themselves?"

"Well, there is one exception."

"What's that?"

"Girls can call old men anything in the book. Be it darling, sugar-pie, baby-kins, doll-cakes, sweetie-pie-facecake, or sweet-whole-pear-in-his-own-heavy-syrup. And old men can use sweet-names in return."

"But, that goes against everything you just said. I don't understand."

He winked. "When you're an old man you will."

LILITH

Sister Lilith. That was my great aunt's name. I didn't know her by any other title. What I did know, is she'd been a nun since nineteen. Sister Lilith shocked my family when she left her convent at the age of forty-four.

She moved in with her partner, Sister Maria.

Together, they bought a small cabin on the lake. Complete with a small speedboat. And no matter how hard they tried, they never got their poor uncoordinated nephew to stand up on a pair of water skis.

And Lord, how they tried.

Both Sister Lilith and Sister Maria helped run a Catholic halfway house for abused women. They even brought troubled ladies home with them for weekends on the lake. They'd let me play Scrabble with them, and they'd kick my tail like two heifers with big vocabularies.

Vociferously.

When Sister Lilith died, my family boycotted her funeral. Staunch German Catholics can be like that, Godless creatures, when they want to be.

Only one of my cousins attended, besides me. The chapel was filled with women. And if you've ever been in a funeral parlor full of abused ladies, you know how many tears were shed. After a series of Latin chants, Sister Maria got up to say a few words.

"This woman was my family," Sister Maria nodded toward the casket. "My own flesh and blood. Even though this world didn't understand us – our own church didn't understand us. I hope our Lord did."

That was all Sister Maria said.

And by God, I think it was enough.

LAUNDRY DAY

My very first fight was over laundry.

As a boy, my mother used a clothesline just like anyone else. It was my job to fold clean laundry, but I was worthless as a can of pumpkin.

Not much has changed.

You could set your watch by Mother's weekly laundering schedule. Tuesdays, Wednesdays, and Thursdays. Never Mondays, Fridays, or Saturdays. And God forbid Sundays. We weren't even allowed to use the bathroom on the Lord's Day.

Much less fish.

The boys behind my house, the Grimshaws, were little heathens. Spencer and his brother Marie-James. Marie-James' mother named him that because she believed she was pregnant with a girl. When he turned out to be a boy, she slapped a masculine name on the end, and ruined that poor boy's life. Some folks called him M.J. for short.

Most called him something more colorful.

One summer day, I caught the Grimshaw boys

stealing from our clothesline in the backyard. My mother's unmentionable garments. I tore off the back porch and threatened to make them very sorry. Marie-James laughed at me, so I made a clever remark about his God-given name. One thing led to another, and somehow, he managed to fit my mother's panties over my head.

Then he beat me into a seedless orange.

When my mother found me lying in the backyard, I was a mess. She dabbed my face with a wet rag.

"God Almighty," she sighed. "Maybe this'll finally teach you to fold the damn laundry from now on."

Then she laughed.

That woman knew me better than that.

COMPUTER LESSONS

We finally bought Jamie's mother a new computer. Not just a computer, a top-of-the-line desktop packed with enough memory to cure Alzheimer's. We mortgaged our washing machine to buy it. The saleswoman asked if we wanted to add a two hundred dollar protection plan. I asked if they sold a twenty dollar plan.

The saleswoman handed me a roll of duct tape.

The truth is, Mary was overdue for a new computer. Her last machine was a khaki-colored relic from '91 that still needed frequent oil changes. The old thing had no modem, but it did have a mouse. The little guy had built a nest right inside the hard drive.

When I unboxed the new computer, I knew we were in for a long, stressful night. At the age of seventy-five, Mary wasn't up to snuff on some basic computer skills – like hearing. It took three hours of instruction just to check the weather.

Then, Mary wanted to do a Google search for her old college pal, Harry Wiener. I couldn't stop her in time.

We saw Harry all right. He looked younger than Mary remembered him.

When we concluded our exhausting lesson, there was one final thing my mother-in-law wanted to learn.

"I want you to put me on MyFace," Mary stated.

"Ma'am," I asked. "MyFace?"

Mary used the wrong words, but I knew what she meant. And to tell you the truth, it wasn't a bad idea.

So, I poured us two stiff whiskeys.

I don't know about her, but after two drinks I was on my face nearly all night.

HER NAME IS PURDY

"I sell commercial air filters," the man told me. "All kinds, I travel all over the South."

Well, it wasn't exactly the most exciting conversation I've ever had. But in Molino, Florida, I've had worse.

Out of the man's truck hobbled a dog. The old girl limped up to me, panting from the effort. She was elderly, too old to wag her tail. Elderly dogs don't waste energy wagging.

Instead, they just smile.

The old girl's name was Purdy. She greeted me by licking my ear. I nearly gagged. Purdy needed a big handful of prescription-strength Tic-Tacs.

Purdy is fourteen years old – eighty-eight in dog years. The man bought her after a nasty divorce. She was his first dog. And he lucked out, she's a good apple. Purdy rides shotgun with him wherever he goes. He even took her to Europe once. She flew in the cargo hold of the plane. Without tranquilizers.

"She's having a rough time," the man explained. "Just found out she's got bladder cancer." He whispered, "It's not good."

The cancer had already spread to Purdy's bones. The vet prescribed meds to make her more comfortable, but mostly she was groggy. She had about four months left.

Maybe less.

The man rubbed her ears. "Shoot, I didn't think the old girl would want to ride in the truck today. Thought the pain meds made her too sleepy. Guess I was wrong."

I'm glad he was.

The day Purdy passes up a truck ride is a day I don't want to think about.

RC COLA

"I like RC Cola from a glass bottle," the boy said. "It tastes better, somehow."

I'll call him Sam, but that's not his real name. Sam is eleven years young. Yesterday, we fished together for three hours while he sipped RC Cola. Sam claimed he was an expert fisherman. He swore he'd caught a six-foot long mahi-mahi once on that little Walmart rod of his.

I pretended to believe him.

When he asked me what I did for a living, I told him I was an Iraqi oil prince who lived aboard a yacht.

Two can play at Sam's game.

Sam and I became fast friends. He's sharp as a razor, but one thing was clear: he hadn't fished before. Not ever. He wasn't even using bait.

Finally, Sam bit the bullet and asked for help.

So, I configured his rod while he told me about himself. Sam's parents are divorced. His two brothers are grown, his sister is too young to play with, and his mother works. His daddy lives in Tennessee, Sam hasn't seen him in three years.

Truth be told, I think Sam's lonely.

Yesterday, his mother unplugged his Xbox and sent him outside to get some sunshine. So, Sam hiked through the woods with his cooler of soda looking for a fishing spot.

I handed him the baited rod, Sam thanked me by offering me an RC Cola.

"You know," he admitted. "I lied earlier, I'm not actually a fisherman."

I patted his shoulder. "You're as much a fisherman as anyone I know."

PAPERBOYS

My first cellphone was a Nokia. An ugly thing with a wrist-strap. I never understood those straps. Never once did I see anyone carry their ten-pound clunker with a wrist-strap.

But I hardly used the phone, it was only for emergencies.

One such emergency took place at four o'clock in the morning. I was delivering three hundred morning newspapers to a high-rise condo on the beach. Twenty-nine floors. I happened upon a drunk woman in the stairwell of the fourteenth floor.

She was bleeding like an upside-down rabbit.

I used my new cellphone to dial 911, then I sat beside her. The woman didn't even know she was injured, she was too busy singing Aretha Franklin songs in her stupor.

When the medics arrived she swatted at them. "Don't touch me!" she yelled. "Don't you know who I am?"

Apparently not.

She laughed. "I'm the Queen of Soul, dammit!"

The medics showed her all the R-E-S-P-E-C-T they could muster, but she was too tanked to notice. They finally loaded her into the ambulance while she belted out another chorus of an Aretha anthem.

Turns out, my cellphone saved the woman's life. The medics said if she'd laid there any longer, she would've bled to death by the third verse. But Lady Soul didn't feel any gratitude toward me.

She dog-cussed me from inside the ambulance.

Later that week, I figured out why. While on my paper-route, I noticed a section on the front page that caught my eye.

The article headline read: "Deliveryman rescues state representative's drunk wife."

JULY FOURTH

We coasted our U-Haul into Florida, mid-afternoon on the Fourth of July. The first thing my mother did was eat a grouper sandwich. No beach, no fireworks. Her first move as a new Floridian would be wolfing down a slab of fish on a toasted bun.

The first thing you should know is, my mother grew up seventeen hours from the Gulf of Mexico. Fresh-caught saltwater fish was something she'd only heard about. She'd tried to persuade Daddy to take a Florida vacation, but it never happened. He wasn't about to drive all that distance just to eat a piece of fish and look at "a bunch of damn water."

So, for her birthday, Daddy took her to Red Lobster. It was a sorry substitute. They didn't even serve grouper there. She settled for the meager Gulf-Shrimp Platter.

And it was as close as she ever got to the Emerald Coast.

After Daddy died, Mother's world went to hell in a bucket. She was a wreck. Sometimes she'd sit in her room for days on end, curled up in that chair of hers, like a ghost. She could go a week without talking if she wanted to. And often did.

But on that Fourth of July, we were new people. Floridians. And Floridians eat grouper sandwiches. I watched Mother eat her first one, it was an enormous hunk of fish. She almost dislocated her jaw getting a bite. Then, she did something I hadn't seen her do in a long time.

She half smiled.

We've eaten grouper every Fourth of July since.

ZIG

Years ago, I met motivational speaker Zig Ziglar. It was at a conference, with an auditorium full of people. We in the audience participated in Zig's exercises, guaranteed to either make us happy or rich.

But never both.

One such activity involved writing a letter to the sixteen-year-old version of ourselves. Turns out, old Zig liked mine the best. He asked me to read it aloud before three hundred of his fans. Here's how it went:

> Dear Sean,
> How've you been, you handsome devil?
> Listen up: in a few years, you'll find yourself in an establishment outside Geneva, Alabama. Some joker will pick a fight with you. He's ugly, and answers to the name J.R. Whatever you do, don't mention the Auburn-Alabama game or he'll beat you like a bare-assed ape. As an addendum, don't dance with any ladies in the aforementioned beer-joint.

One of them is J.R.'s girlfriend.

Moving right along. When driving down the highway, always watch for roadsigns marked, "fresh asphalt." I know it's ridiculous. But it turns out, deputies take these signs very seriously.

So do county judges.

On another matter: if you find yourself at a swanky cocktail party with your wife, don't let your buddy Andrew fix you a drink. Also, don't incite the crowd to sing Sweet Caroline. It's tacky. And no matter how Andrew insists, never attempt to breakdance. Ever. The mayor happens to be at one of these parties, and your wife Jamie will disown you.

She will leave the party without you.

Your cellphone will be dead.

And it's a nine-mile march back home.

ATARI NIGHTS

My daddy hated video games. He had an outdated fear of them. "They're a waste of time," he'd say. "They'll rot your brain to the core." He said it so often I believed it.

Subsequently, video games terrified me. I thought if I looked upon Pac-Woman's round figure for even a moment, my brain would trickle out my ears.

I was still willing to take the chance though.

When my buddy Larry got an Atari 5200 console for his birthday, he invited me to play it. I warned Larry that our brains would turn into urinal cakes if we touched the thing. But Larry was a gambler by nature.

We played for five hours.

That year for my birthday, I asked Daddy for an Atari 5200. He didn't even acknowledge the question. He just looked at me with sad eyes, like I'd just used an ugly word. I knew how he felt about video games. I had a better chance of getting a jug of Jack Daniels for my birthday.

Neither of us mentioned the issue again.

The day of my birthday, I arrived home from school to an empty house. Nobody was in the kitchen, the lights were all off. When I walked down the basement stairs, I was greeted with a "Surprise!"

And it was a surprise. Mother and Daddy stood in front of a small upright piano, all wrapped up with a big ribbon.

Daddy grinned. "The way I see it, your friends will outgrow their video games," he said. "But you'll be playing one of these until you're old and gray."

If he could only see me now.

KENDALL'S BARBECUE

I ate lunch at Kendall's Barbecue joint in Georgiana, Alabama. On the bench next to me sat a talkative elderly man named Byron. I was so mesmerized by his stories, I even flipped out my phone audio recorder.

Here's what he had to say:

"See," Byron began. "Hank Williams and my oldest sister went to school together, just up the road."

"Hank Williams?" I asked.

"The one and only," he said. "My sister fancied herself a musician. She was just about the most horrible thing you ever heard. She played the spoons – and sang too. If you could call it singing."

"When she was sixteen, Hank's band stopped through Georgiana. They held a concert down at the Ga-Ana Theatre." He pointed out the window. "Just down yonder."

"So, my sister asked Hank if she could sing and play a few tunes with the band. If you can believe it, Hank agreed to let her." Byron winked. "Hank didn't know nothing about her singing, he only let her onstage because she cut a fine figure."

Byron made the shape of an hourglass with his hands.

"Well, the joke was on old Hank," he said. "When she opened her mouth, everyone cringed. She howled a stanza of Jesus Paid it All. Folks shook their heads, wishing Jesus would've only paid half."

He thumped his hand on the table. "She's the only person in the world who ever upstaged Hank Williams."

Finally I interrupted, "What year did this happen?"

Byron patted my shoulder. "Hell, I don't remember. Truth is, I don't even have a sister."

BOILED PEANUTS

Outside Robertsdale, Alabama is a highway market with the best boiled peanuts you've ever tasted. Cajun style. I first tried them several years ago, on one of the worst weeks of my life

Let me back up. At the time, I worked as a delivery van driver. My supervisor, a hateful little snot who ironed his jeans and spoke with a nasal voice, was named Roger.

Roger informed me he was decreasing my pay, the company had fallen on hard times. But it gets worse. The following Wednesday my cocker spaniel died. I woke up to find her curled up at the foot of my bed.

The lowest blow came on Friday. While making deliveries in the eastern tip of Alabama, the transmission on my delivery van died.

The vehicle broke down just outside Robertsdale. I coasted into the little roadside market and called Roger on the company cellphone. I explained what happened, and he cussed me out for missing my deliveries.

Then Roger up and fired me, right there. Over the

phone.

I fell into a state of shock. I wandered into the market and loaded up two bagfuls of boiled peanuts. The woman behind the counter gave me one of those looks.

"You okay sweetie?" she asked.

"I don't know." I sighed. "You ever feel like the world is against you, like nobody cares?"

Then, I choked on my words and started crying.

Without saying a thing, she came around the counter and pulled me into herself. We stood there for five minutes. Two perfect strangers, embracing.

"Well, I care," she said.

She didn't charge me for the peanuts.

GREEN THUMBS

My wife has a green thumb. She can grow almost anything by taking a clipping. The woman could plant bacon in the dirt, and in a few months we'd have a baby sow wandering around the backyard. I don't have that talent. I tried to plant an empty can of beer once. Nothing happened. I also tried planting a dollar bill.

The next day, the dollar had turned into three quarters.

Jamie's a thief about plant clippings. Her favorite thing to do is to visit places with lots of plants. Then, when no one's looking, she pinches one leaf from the stem and hides it in her purse. It's unethical, but she's been doing it for years. In fact, every plant we have in our house is an illegal clone.

She's never bought a single one.

They all come from clippings.

You want succulents? We have thousands. Creeping Pliea, or Sweedish Ivy? We have so much I'm afraid it's going to strangle me in the night and steal all my beer.

Yesterday, I was in the hardware store buying

lightbulbs. Across the store, I spotted a familiar face in the garden section. It was Jamie. I saw her pinch a leaf from a potted plant. I busted her cold.

"Jamie Dietrich," I scolded. "Open up your purse."

She refused.

So, I grabbed at her purse. "You've got to stop this behavior. It's wrong."

Jamie screamed at the top of her lungs, "Thief! Help! He's trying to steal my purse. Someone stop this man!"

And that's exactly what the manager did.

BURRITOS

For lunch yesterday, I ordered a burrito that was the size of a Cadillac. And it dawned on me, food portions have gotten bigger over the years.

When I was growing up, there never seemed to be enough food. Take McDonald's for instance: their hamburgers used to be paper-thin patties on Styrofoam buns. Along with your meal you'd get six french fries, and one squirt of ketchup.

Everything was smaller back then. Remember McDonald's tiny ice cream cones? You took three licks, and you were already down to the cone.

These days, things are nice and big. McDonald's has enlarged everything, they've even upstaged the Happy Meal – thank God. Now they have something called the Mighty Kids Meal. It's mighty alright. It comes with a half-pound burger, fries, nuggets, egg salad, a wedge of birthday cake, a Budweiser, and an iPad.

Perhaps the most heroic food portions are found at Chipotle Mexican Grill. Yesterday, a server was wrapping my herculean burrito when the tortilla broke.

"Whoops," she said. "You want me to add another tortilla?"

It sounded plausible.

She blessed me with another dollop of guacamole and wrapped my wounded burrito with a second tortilla. It tore again.

Third time's a charm.

She added two more tortillas. By then, my burrito resembled a newborn hog wrapped in a swaddling parka. For my trouble, she threw in some napkins and a free syringe of insulin.

I've never been so excited to eat in my life. But, something didn't seem quite right. I inspected my bag.

She forgot my damn chips.

RIGHT ON TARGET

In Target, a group of teenage girls stood in the checkout line next to Jamie and me. They were rowdy tourists and giggled at everything. Two of the girls played an impromptu game of tag, the other four took turns seeing who could burp the loudest.

The brunette won.

On the conveyor belt, I counted six boxes of cheap wine, stacked up like a pyramid. It wasn't the good kind of wine, but the cheap kind they serve prison inmates.

The cashier looked at the wine. "I need to see some ID," she said.

The brunette rummaged through her purse. She handed a card to the cashier.

The cashier squinted at the ID and made a face. "This isn't you," she said. "It doesn't even look like you."

"Of course it's me," the girl insisted. "That's my driver's license."

The cashier wasn't buying it. "Oh yeah? When's your birthday then?"

"My birthday?"

"That's right."

The girl scoffed. "This is ridiculous. Let me have my license back."

But the cashier would do no such thing. "I asked you when your birthday was."

The girl let out a sigh, then thought for a moment. "April thirty-first?"

The cashier handed the ID back. "Go put all this damn alcohol back where it came from before I call my supervisor."

With frowns on their faces, the underaged girls took the boxes of wine and sulked away. And just like that, they were gone.

"Dumb tourists." The cashier shook her head. "The month of April only has thirty days in it."

"Hussies," Jamie mumbled under her breath.

Thanks for playing, girls.

WORK FOR YOUR SUPPER

What I hate most about Friday night dinner parties is the dreaded question, "What do you do?" It's a question I've never known exactly how to answer, because I've had too many jobs. So many, in fact, I was recently diagnosed with occupational-schizophrenia by a homeopathic doctor.

The doc wrote me a prescription for a seventy-dollar jar of mud.

And told me to eat it.

Which job is the real me? I've been a landscaper, a tile-layer, a cabinet-builder, a deliveryman, a paperboy, a power-washer, a house framer, an electrician's assistant, a sailboat deckhand, a hay baler, a brick mason, a refrigerator mover, a retail specialist, a trim carpenter, a cook, a fry-cook, a dishwasher, a sheetrocker, a lifeguard, an oyster-shucker, a tomato-picker, and a condo cleaner. I was even an ordained minister for nineteen days – before they took me to small claims court.

People love to ask each other what they do for a

living. It's a standard question. Along with, "How many kids do you have?" or my personal favorite, "How much do you earn annually – after taxes?"

But, if you suffer from multiple-profession-personality disorder, such questions are uncomfortable.

Long ago, I decided to respond with creative answers. I've come up with some zingers too. I've told people I'm everything from a proctologist to a production supervisor for The Bachelor. Once, I even claimed to be the dean of Harvard – that was a wedding toast I had no business making. But my favorite answer is one I learned from a sixteen-year-old with dreadlocks and body odor.

Here's how it goes:

"So," someone asked him. "What do you do?"

"Do?" he answered. "About what?"

UNCLE JOHN

Uncle John liked to claim he was a classical guitarist, and he'd say it without a hint of irony. Then, he and Grandaddy would play Waltz Across Texas, howling in twangy voices. When finished, John would say, "If that ain't a classical tune, I don't know what is."

Grandaddy taught Uncle John everything he knew.

For two years, Uncle John lived in an RV on the back edge of our farm. I don't think I ever saw him dressed in anything but overalls and a T-shirt. It was all he wore. Of course, there's not much else to wear working at a fertilizer plant.

I saw my uncle in the mornings for breakfast, and in the evenings for supper. The old boy never missed a meal. And he must've had a million and one jokes to his name, because he had a new one every morning.

His inappropriate ones were masterpieces

In John's RV, he kept a guitar and accordion. When he finished guitar, he'd switch instruments and squeeze out music my grandaddy once taught him to play. Melodies like, 'O Sole Mio, or Bella Napoli. Between tunes, he'd pause and tell me his half-true stories. Tall tales designed to make me either laugh or gasp.

Sometimes both.

Of course, I also remember the morning John came to the front door dressed in a suit. It was a strange sight, he looked ridiculous. He never used the front door, and he certainly never wore neckties.

But then, you don't wear jeans to sing at your own daddy's funeral.

THE CLASS OF 2015

The auditorium was nearly empty at Walton Academy's graduation. It took place in DeFuniak Springs, Florida this past weekend.

Not long ago, I'd never even heard of this county school before. It's not a traditional high school. Many of the students hail from Paxton, or Mossy Head. They come from hardworking families, with no means.

The 2015 class was tiny, not enough graduates to form a baseball team. Their ceremony was casual. If you showed up in anything more than a T-shirt, you found yourself overdressed.

Take me, for instance: I was overdressed.

I noticed the graduates weren't taking selfies. A teacher told me it's because most of them don't have cellphones. She said they didn't take senior trips, attend proms, or apply to colleges either. They're too busy with full-time jobs, and newborns.

They're poor.

The teacher went on to say she keeps food in her classroom since the kids don't have enough to eat at home. Charities dole out bags of groceries sometimes. "But you gotta get there early," one student says. "All the bags get snatched quick."

These are Walton county's rejects. They know it too. Most of them don't make it past eighth grade.

But these graduates did.

They were a handsome lot. Under-confident children wearing gowns. The students threw their caps in the air. The thin crowd rose to its feet. The man next to me, still in dirty work clothes, clapped so hard he nearly broke his wrist.

"That's my son," he said.

Yes it was.

It certainly was.

JUNIOR

"Have you seen my momma?" the boy asked.

The little guy was cute as a duck in a hat, wandering around the restaurant.

"No," I said, with a mouthful. "What's she look like?"

He shrugged. "Daddy says she's pretty."

"Nope, definitely haven't seen her."

I told him to have a seat. The boy had the gift of gab, he was so full of wind he could've inflated an onion sack. All he did was talk about his heroic deer-hunting daddy.

Boys do that.

"Is that beer?" he pointed. "My daddy likes beer. He drinks it when he's hunting. He's a sharpshooter, the deer are scared of him. He's the best."

Mazel tov.

Junior dug in his nose. "Are you eating deer?"

"No, catfish."

He wrinkled his face. "Like deer?"

"Exactly like deer."

"Daddy hunts deer. He's gonna take me hunting,

we're gonna pop a whitetail. He's gonna let me shoot it!"

I sure hope everyone wears orange.

Just then, a woman toting a baby walked up. She swatted Junior's hindquarters with a hairbrush. She threatened to flog him and bury him in the parking lot. Junior thought that was marvelous.

"See ya later buddy." I high-fived him. "Hope you have fun hunting with your daddy."

"His daddy?" the woman said. "Is that who he was talking about?" She sighed. "He ain't never even met his daddy. That fool left us before he was born. My boy ain't nothing but a liar."

I grinned at Junior, whose face was red. That poor child isn't a liar.

He just wants to go hunting.

A LITTLE SQUIRRELLY

I'm not sure when I decided I wanted to be reincarnated as a squirrel, but that's what I'd prefer. The subject comes up from time to time during regular discussion. I ought to keep my mouth shut about it, but I don't.

"I'd like to come back as a squirrel," I said once, at a dinner party. The kind of party held in a huge house; with people in linen suits, holding glasses of something that costs more than my health insurance premiums.

My comment was followed by the mysterious disappearance of my wife. Then, a deafening silence fell on the rest of the dinner table – save for the faint creaking of a chair.

The little girl next to me chimed in, "Well, I want to be a turtle." And the entire table cooed with adoration for the freckled philosopher.

"A turtle?" I said. "Turtles couldn't avoid a chubby toddler on the sidewalk dragging a wagon."

The little girl shrugged. "Turtles live to be two hundred."

"Not if they're flattened by a Mazda they don't."

The little girl shook her head. "Statistically speaking, squirrels get hit by more cars than turtles do."

"How could you know that?"

"The internet."

"Who invited you to this party anyway?"

"This is my daddy's house."

"Well, I must say, I absolutely love the outside paved patio."

"The fire pit is a nice touch, no?"

"It really is."

I first decided to revisit earth as a squirrel when I was nine. It happened when a warren of them invaded my uncle's attic. My uncle took two days off work to address the infestation.

His rendezvous involved two-story ladders, cigarettes, twenty-two gauge rifles, cigarettes, wire traps, cigarettes, knee pads, cigarettes, and all the cussing a nine-year-old boy like me could hope for.

My uncle laid on his belly in the attic and whispered, "These goddamn suckers must've been human in a past life, to be so smart. You know, I don't think anything can kill them."

Not true Uncle Frank. It bears mentioning that squirrels have their fair share of predators. Snakes, raccoons, foxes, owls, hawks, weasels, certain varieties of big lizards, house cats, dogs, possums, wild boars, humans, and anything else that has a pulse likely enjoys the taste of squirrel meat. It doesn't end there. Other chipmunk murderers are: cars, busses, trains, high cholesterol, and of course, modernized country music, which is an affront to squirellhood entirely. Still, it beats the hell out of being a turtle, rooting around for worm poop.

Like many who live in my part of the world, I grew up hunting squirrel with my father. We'd pop them in the treetops all day long with a rifle. Most often, we ate them smother-fried. Which means they were battered, deep-fried, re-battered, fried again, then fried a third time in an oily gravy that looks like virgin motor oil. If you've never had such a dish, chances are you speak like someone from New Jersey and say things like, "Aw, so is your old man."

One night, my father brought a bag of squirrels home for dinner. And, in light of my recent convictions on reincarnation, I refused to eat them.

"Why aren't you eating your dinner?" Mother asked.

"I can't eat this. It might be someone's grandma."

She gave me one of those looks. It was the same look she wore when she explained that only girls are supposed to pee sitting down.

"What are you talking about?" my father asked.

I poked the meat with my finger. "This could've been Clyde Schmidt's grandma."

"Old lady Schmidt? Now just wait a damned minute. She died?"

"Yep. Last week."

"I didn't even know she was sick."

"She wasn't, she died of boredom while listening to modern country music."

"Well, I'll be."

"Dad, is it wrong to pee sitting down?"

My mother shot up from the table.

"How about I make some Jell-O? Wouldn't that be nice?"

As time went on, I became so affixed with squirrels that I dreamt about them when I slept. And the pinnacle, of my squirrel-fascination came in the form of a hand puppet. It was a puppet with two big squirrel eyes, and a pair of plastic buck teeth that looked like they could slice through a block of oak. I named my stuffed friend, Ernie.

Ernie and I spent a summer together. He slept beside me, ate meals with me, and even took baths with me. At first, Mother didn't seem to mind her ten-year-old being subjoined to a cotton squirrel. As long as I didn't bring Ernie to supper in the evenings.

But, the winds of Ernie's velvet fate changed one day when he sassed my mother in his little squirrel voice.

She whipped her head around, eyes consumed with fury. "What'd you say to me?" she asked Ernie, steam drifting out of her nostrils.

Ernie said, "I don't want to mow the yard today. I want to read comic books – preferably while drinking a glass of sweet tea."

Oh, how I cringed at Ernie's brash words toward my mother. He had nuts, I'll give him that.

"I see," said Mother. "And what else would Ernie like?"

This was a trap.

"Hmmm," thought Ernie. "How about some fresh-baked cookies?"

"Anything else I could get you? Perhaps I could fetch your slippers and get you a cigar?"

"You're a doll, don't let anyone tell you otherwise."

But it was already too late, Ernie was in the broom closet before he even finished his sentence.

After a cooling off period, Mother came to me and broke the news. "Listen honey, I just spoke with Ernie, and he told me to deliver a message to you."

"He did?"

"Yes, he said he's going on a trip to see the world. Never to return."

"That doesn't sound like Ernie. He hates to fly."

"It's a trip by boat."

"Ernie's terrified of water."

"Well, it's a train, too."

"A train that's also a boat?"

"It floats a little, yes."
"Is it a fast train-boat?"
"Faster than a speeding bullet."
"I've heard of those."

My mother stroked my hair. "It really doesn't matter. Look, I want you to stop playing with Ernie and spend time with kids your own age."

My mother had a point, Ernie was in his early thirties, I was still a boy. He needed to be free to see the world, and by God, I needed to let him go. So, I prayed for his safe travels and bid him goodbye. That might've been the last time I ever saw Ernie, if it wouldn't have been for the annual talent show.

That following year, when the leaves began to fall from the trees, our elementary school held a talent show. It was a longstanding tradition. My father competed in the same talent show when he was a boy.

People from every grade showed up to strut there stuff at the elementary school. Some of the hottest acts in the county included: the Galloway sisters; who each year, executed an annual human-pyramid act, a monumental experience. There was Peter Mills, who did a breakdancing routine to a Strauss waltz; Robbie and his sister Lola with their broadway review – Robbie dressed like a girl, Lola dressed like a Republican donkey; Amber Markson did her legendary impersonation of Eleanor Roosevelt, which always ended with a chorus of the National Anthem; and then there was Gilbert Schoop – who everyone called Poop – the ventriloquist.

Like me, Poop was considered to be a nobody by the upper-crust kids. Meaning, no one paid him any mind unless they needed a roaming spitball target. People like Poop and I maintained our roles in the adolescent caste system, never overstepping those boundaries. Except when it came to the annual talent show. The one and only time in our lives when society gave us permission to sparkle.

And sparkle, Poop did. He was a spectacular showman. He had a cowboy puppet with red hair – reminiscent of Buffalo Bob and Howdy Doody. Just the year before, Poop delivered an onslaught of jokes that left the auditorium in stitches. And for his grand finale, he coaxed his puppet to guzzle a full glass of water. After a trick like that, he received a standing ovation, a champagne shower in his dressing room, and the key to the city.

I was determined to beat Poop at his own game. It was to be my year to outshine the king himself. After reading a book on ventriloquism, I practiced throwing my voice for hours. And it's not as easy as it sounds. I rehearsed day and night with my puppet Ernie, who was suffering from a critical case of jet-lag.

I tried my routine out on my mother. It went like this:

"Good evening ladies and germs. This is my worthy constituent, Ernie. Say hello Ernie."

"Hello Ernie," he said in a nasal voice.

"What's new, Ernie?"

"Not much. Say, did you hear the doctor gave me only six months to live?"

"Oh my, that's terrible."

"Yeah, but I couldn't pay the bill so I got another six months."

My mother cleared her throat. "Honey, am I supposed to see your mouth moving?"

"Moving? You can see it moving?"

She nodded.

"Ernie," I said through clenched teeth. "Tell us about your dog."

"Well, I have a dog named Rex, and he br–"

"Wait," my mother interrupted. "The squirrel has a dog?"

"Yes, he has a dog."

"Okay. That's a little strange don't you think?"

"No. I have a dog."

"But you're not a squirrel."

"That's because I'm not dead yet. No more interruptions."

Ernie continued, "My dog Rex brings the paper every morning, he's a very talented dog. But I've trained him to do something even better. I stuff a five-dollar bill into his collar, and send him to the store for groceries."

"That's fantastic, Ernie."

"Yesterday, I stuffed more money than usual in his collar. He left like usual. And he was gone all day."

"What happened?"

"I tracked him down. I finally found him in town sniffing a female dog, behaving very indecently. So, I asked him why he was behaving in such an immoral manner, since he'd never acted that way before."

"What'd he say?"

"Rex told me it was because he'd never had money before."

Silence from my audience.

"Well Mother," I said. "What do you think?"

She stood up. "What would you think if I made us a big bowl of Jell-O? Wouldn't that be nice?"

I hung my head.

Hell yes it'd be nice.

On the day of the talent show, I arrived to the auditorium dressed in a suit finished, with a yellow bow-tie. I was nervous as a gnat in a car. I watched Poop do his routine onstage. He was in top form that year, the best shape of his life. Poop stunned the audience with new material and flawless vocal technique. His coup de grâce was a song and dance number to Barbara Streisand's "People." The audience nearly tore the room apart.

My mother stood beside me backstage. "He was good," she said.

"He's more than that," I answered. "He's a genius."

"You know, you don't have to go through with this."

"But wouldn't that make me a quitter?"

"No." She smoothed her dress. "It means that I'll take you out for ice cream."

"Huh?"

"You heard me. As much ice cream as you can shove down your fat little gullet if you don't go out there and do that thing with your puppet."

"Thing with my puppet?"

"And ten dollars."

"But..."

"Alright, fifteen. But you have to promise to start peeing standing up."

Don't be ridiculous.

As an adult, I feel it's important to believe something about the afterlife. Whether that belief is true or not doesn't matter to me. The world is a hateful place sometimes, and I'd like to think something better awaits us. Something better than this.

Maybe nothing happens when we die. Maybe we're laid in soil and become worm poop. That's what a college professor once told me. "Modern science," he said, "says everything either becomes worm poop, or fish poop in the end. Sometimes both."

Well maybe that's true. God knows, modern country music is already halfway there.

Most people I know think Christianity has been right all along. Maybe they're right. God-willing, some of us will float upward to heaven like my grandmother once believed. Maybe we'll all be welcomed by a Walmart greeter at the gates, handed white choir robes and fliers for real estate. Maybe we'll play a few tunes on the harp, like "Old Rugged Cross," or "Peace in the Valley."

Maybe I'll see my grandmother again. I could think of worse things than a hyper-religious afterlife.

But sometimes, I watch squirrels leap from limb to limb outside. Fast little creatures. They never pause to worry about mortgages or life insurance premiums. They don't have cellphones, cable television, or Tylenol. They don't need any of it. Hell, maybe they've had all those things once before.

And then, I wonder if human beings are as supreme as we've been told we are. Maybe the highest level of consciousness isn't humanity at all. Perhaps, destroying the world with bombs and bad country music is actually the *lowest* level of consciousness the world has ever seen. Maybe happiness is being a squirrel. Flying from branch to branch.

One of God's many creatures that pee sitting down.

THIS MUCH I KNOW IS TRUE

It's wrong to lie. I know that. As a boy, my struggle was telling the truth without frills or decoration, to make it prettier.

It was difficult as a child, I'll admit. Because the Good Lord gave me an extraordinary gift for falsity. Though my mother never called it lying, she called it "telling stories." My friends referred to a well-told lie as, "bull." The pastor called dishonesty, "bearing false witness." My father called it "crusing-for-a-god-damn-licking."

As a boy, Mother suggested I focus my talents onto paper. And for the most part, it aided in sufficing my creative needs. I burned off excess energy by crafting cute stories about pirates, girls, and baseball.

It was a good idea on her part. By writing, I didn't have to lie about feeding the chickens or cutting the grass, when really, I was burying a case of beer behind the goat pen with a shovel. As a fifteen-year-old boy, I laid claim to the largest stash of beer in three counties. Among my friends, I was known as William Shakes-Beer. Several cases of beer laid piled up in a hole large enough to fit a Buick. Much of it still remains beneath the fertile soil to this day. I suppose, years after I'm deceased, future archeologists will find my stash of beer – along with an assortment of cheap cigars – and they will bless my memory for it.

For me, not embellishing became harder when girls entered my life. I wanted them to like me. It was only natural. The fact was, girls were fickle. Sometimes they needed convincing. For instance: I concocted a small story to persuade Rachel Simms into romance when I was eleven. I told Rachel I was going to be launched into outer space in a rocket ship.

Rachel balked at such a claim. She was smarter than the average astronaut. But I insisted my story was true. I explained I'd been selected in a nationwide search, along with nine other future-cosmonauts, commissioned by the president himself to accompany Giggles – the world's first astronaut-raccoon – into space. When I showed Rachel the fake NASA photo ID I'd ordered from the back of a Popular Mechanics Magazine, she pretended to believe me.

Of course, Rachel knew it was a lie. "There probably never was a Giggles the raccoon," she said later. "You made that up too, didn't you?"

Nope. Think again sister.

Giggles was real, but he was no astronaut. Giggles used to dig through our garbage can at night, eating old coffee grounds and Kleenex. I named him that because each morning, Daddy would say the same thing. "That coon is probably watching me clean up his mess, just goddamn giggling the whole time."

Still, the lies flowed from my mouth like creek water.

Let me introduce you to Kylie Hart. Kylie was a gifted violinist, with long brown hair, and two dolloped eyes that were as black as the kind of chocolate you get in boxes. She was nearly perfect.

I asked Kylie to go to the movies with me. She

refused. So, I asked her to go roller-skating. Again she refused. I upped the stakes and told her I was a five-time winner of the Little-League World Series. She wished me well in the upcoming playoffs, and warned me against blood doping.

Which does not exist in baseball, Kylie.

I wasn't about to give up, even though Kylie turned me down over twenty times. I finally won her over when I casually mentioned that I was a budding classical violinist. Oh heaven have mercy on me, it was a downright blatant lie – the only kind worth telling. The truth was, in fact, the only violin I'd ever even seen was my uncle John's ratty old fiddle.

"Are you fooling me?" Kylie said. "You're a violinist?"

"Yes, but I prefer to call myself a humble disciple of Bach and Vivaldi."

"Disciple?"

Maybe I was laying it on a little too thick.

She asked, "How long have you played?"

"Well, not long enough to make the maple sing the unslaked words of my restless heart and soul."

Kylie touched her chest.

Eat your heart out William Shakes-Beer.

"Kylie," I said. "I just want to make what's in here..." I tapped my sternum, "...get out into the world. Tell me, Kylie, do you ever wake up in the morning, and find yourself yearning for something un-nameable?"

"Oh yes. But that's art isn't it? Naming the things our celestial universe has left unnamed."

"Uh, right."

My false story worked. That next weekend, I found myself with Kylie sitting in a dark movie theatre. The weekend afterward, at a fast-food pizza restaurant. The weekend after, Kylie and I went to an amusement park.

One day, at Kylie's house, her father came to me and

said, "I understand you play violin."

"I forgot to mention," Kylie whispered to me. "Daddy's a classical violinist. He's very good."

"It's true." he winked. "I almost majored in violin in college, but it was too much work, I went for something easier."

"Easier?"

"Aeronautical Spacecraft Engineering."

"You must know Giggles then."

"Who?"

"Never mind."

He winked twice. "Look, I'd love to hear you play. I don't meet many kids interested in Bach." He winked again.

When I got home that night, I asked my Father if he had any Bach records. "Bach?" he said. "How many years Bach do you want to go?" To which he laughed and laughed.

Enter my uncle John, who lived in an RV on the edge of our land. He was the only man who played the fiddle that I knew of. Uncle John wore a long walrus mustache, owned one pair of overalls, and drank beer like it sweet tea. I explained to him my problem.

"Gee." Uncle John stroked his chin. "I'd like to help you impress your lady, buddy, but the truth is, I can't teach you to play the the fiddle."

"Why not?"

"It ain't because I don't want to. It's because I ain't got no fiddle. I lost it in Savannah on a bet. Damn Navy boys."

"I'm screwed."

"No you ain't, we just need to visit a pawn shop's all."

John was a citizen of the world. A man with answers. There are too few of them in this life.

"Go home," John explained. "Find something to hock. And whatever you do, don't mention my name, especially not to your momma. Tell a fib if you have to."

"But Uncle John, isn't it wrong to lie?"

And then we both laughed until we pissed our pants.

I went home and scavenged through the attic for something of value. I ended up trading in an old corroded tuba at the local pawn-shop. The man looked at it and said, "Hmm, this ain't stolen, is it?"

"Stolen? Who goes around stealing tubas?"

"You'd be surprised. I once had a man try to hawk his mother's casket."

"How? What about his mother?"

"Oh her? She just laid there, didn't say much of nothing."

He sold me my first fiddle. It had two cigarette burns on the face, a scratched up case, and only two strings. Uncle John, balanced the weathered instrument low on his shoulder and tuned it.

"Uncle John, do you know classical music?"

"You goddamn bet I do, I know about every one of them songs there ever was." Uncle John wasted no time, he bowed out a few bars of "Waltz Across Texas."

"But, you said you knew classical."

"Son, if that ain't one of the greatest classics that there ever was, I'll eat my hat."

It sounded reasonable.

That night, I sat in Uncle John's RV learning Ernest Tubbs' pièce de résistance, while John plowed through a six-pack. He bargained with me. For each wrong note I played, I owed him a beer. After several hours of practice, I owed John nearly eight hundred thousand beers.

A few weeks went by, Uncle John taught me a few more songs in the same manner: "Walking the Floor Over You," "Turkey in the Straw," and "Hello Trouble Come on In." It was evident I'd never impress the symphony orchestra, though my Uncle believed I might have a future in beer joints if I stuck to it.

My fateful moment came while I visited at Kylie's house one evening. Her father went and retrieved a fine handcrafted Spanish violin from a climate controlled closet. He unlatched its case, and with surgical carefulness, removed the instrument. He handed it to me with unwavering trust, then winked three times.

Kylie later explained to me those weren't winks. Her father had been diagnosed with a twitching eyelid that was bad to act up whenever he got dehydrated.

I held the violin on my shoulder and closed my eyes. Then, I imagined the crippling disappointment that was about to follow. Still, the more I thought about it, the more I believed I deserved humiliation. Because in truth, lying is a horrid thing, and those who engage in it should be horsewhipped.

I bowed the strings, playing through the twangy hillbilly music I'd practiced for so many hours. And of course, like my Uncle John taught me, I sang along. With every drop of sincerity I had in me, so help me, I sang.

When the music ended, I opened my eyes. Everyone stared at me with big eyes.

Kylie's father said to her, winking. "Go upstairs and fetch your violin."

"My violin?" she asked.

Her father looked at me, he winked eight times. "Tonight we're going to have a hoedown. You didn't tell me this boy knew the good old classics."

And well.

I never told another lie after that.

Never.

A FEMA TRAILER FOR MOTHER

"Honey, you should know I've filed for bankruptcy," Mother said, shoveling sausage gravy onto my biscuit. Then she held up the pitcher. "More juice?" She topped off my glass without waiting for my answer.

Her words hit me like a slap with a baseball mitt. I stopped eating. "Mother, what'd you just say?"

"I asked if you wanted orange juice."

"No, before that."

Her face grew solemn, and she hung her head. "I'm bankrupt," she admitted. Mother collapsed in her chair and explained the entire situation. She told me about the credit cards, and her herculean IRS debt. And then, my silver-haired mother buried her face in her hands and started crying.

I suppose the first thing you ought to know about my mother is that she doesn't cry. She's an experienced optimist. In fact, I've seen her cry only twice in my entire life. Once, when a bumblebee flew into her ear canal and stung her eardrum. The other time was when Conway Twitty died.

My mother didn't even weep at my father's funeral. Oh, she could have, but she chose not to – for my sake. During his visitation service, Mother stood before the casket with a stiff spine, pumping every damn hand offered to her. And when they took him away, she remained composed while I cried into her skirt.

"The landlord is kicking me out," Mother said.

"When?"

"Two days ago." My mother wiped her tears and pushed her plate toward me. "I'm not hungry. You want my biscuit, honey? I made them fresh this morning."

I stared at my small, red-faced mother, who was staring back at me. There were no two ways about it.

Of course I wanted her biscuit.

~

The Craigslist ad advertised a "Thirty-foot mansion with clean refrigerator and barely-used toilet. MUST SEE TO BELIEVE!" It was the lowest-priced travel trailer in three states. And after an all-night drive to New Orleans, I understood why.

The skinny man gave me the dime tour of his dilapidated FEMA trailer. He showed me the queen bed, the soft spot on the floor, and the mostly mold-free sofa. The mobile paradise had seen better days.

Finally, the man led me into the bathroom to demonstrate the flushing mechanism on the trailer's pièce de résistance. When he bent over, I noticed a handgun tucked in the waist of his trousers. I decided not to bargain on the asking price since pristine toilets were hard to come by.

When I drew up the bill of sale, I asked, "Do you have the official title to this trailer?"

"Lucy." He grinned his three teeth at me. "Her official title is: Lady Lucy of the Crescent City."

I glanced at his pistol and told him it was a lovely title.

After securing Lady Lucy to my truck hitch, I bid New Orleans goodbye and set off for home. I bounded out of the lowlands, watching the bayous zip past my windshield at 70 miles per hour. For the first part of my drive, things went well.

But when I hit Carriere, Mississippi, everything changed.

I heard an explosion. Immediately, my steering wheel jerked left, and I shot across the highway. In the heat of the moment, I tried to scream an ugly word, but all I could get out was, "Mother FEMA!" Muscling my truck onto the shoulder of the highway was like trying to land a wingless 747 without Jesus.

After spending the day in Pearl River County, mortgaging my liver to buy tires, I spent the night on Lady Lucy's musty sofa. It smelled like a robust bouquet of cat piss and Cheetos.

The next morning, I was back on the interstate with renewed energy. By the time I hit Enterprise, Mississippi, I felt more relaxed. I thought about Mother, how much she'd sacrificed during my childhood. I remembered the night shifts she worked, the clothes she made for us, and her biscuits.

By Greene County, Alabama, I was singing along with Conway Twitty on the radio, the way Mother would've done. And it was during the second chorus of "Hello Darlin'," that something in the side mirror caught my eye.

I leaned in for a closer look.

A white FEMA-trailer door was turning somersaults behind me, in the middle of I-59. A chorus of screeching tires and blaring horns serenaded the door's magnificent journey across the highway. The airborne obelisk finally touched down beneath an oncoming sixteen-wheeler. I let out a sigh and did what anyone else in my position would've done.

I turned up the radio.

~

After three years, Mother's trailer still looks as god-awful as ever. But she likes it. And her backyard tomato garden is downright impressive. That's where she spends most of her time, with her vegetables. Her garden is made from tractor tires that pepper her lawn in a semi-circle.

There, Mother does battle with local squirrels over the legal rights to her tomatoes. Her defense is an old-fashioned pesticide made of Red Man chew and water. In the afternoons, you can see squirrels relaxing high in the trees, spitting.

The covered wooden porch that leads into Lady Lucy is six feet high. I should know, I built it. Mother has decorated Lucy's interior with curtains and frilly throw pillows. Somehow, she's managed to transform the ambulatory Katrina-shelter into a home fit for company. That woman.

With enough throw pillows, she could make the morgue look good.

Sometimes, Mother invites our family over for supper. We eat outdoors, by her garden. She can do more in her tiny kitchen than most people do with a thousand dollars and a Bible. She cooks butterbeans, pan-fried chicken and sourdough biscuits big enough to use in pillow fights.

If you wander into her bedroom, on her nightstand you'll see a photograph from the day of my wedding. In the picture, a tall, awkward groom stands next to her wearing a stupid grin. Mother is five feet high, able to fit her head into the notch beneath his arm. She's looking upward at him. He looks uncomfortable in that tuxedo.

Not much has changed. I still look bad in tuxes, and Mother still doesn't have any money. The truth is, she probably never will. But she's got me, damn it. And that's all I care about

Well.

I also care a great deal for her biscuits.

ME IN MY OWN WORDS

As a child, I liked to write. I filled up notebooks with tales of the high-seas, shameless vixens, and steamy scenarios combining both of the aforementioned. My fifth grade teacher found one of my notebooks and scanned through it. She told me I wrote with too many commas, and encouraged me to pursue a career in construction work.

That, old, woman, never, liked, me.

Years later, I learned my teacher had left the school. She took a job at the Piggly Wiggly as a cashier. I went to visit the old girl, to show her the man I'd grown into.

She seemed genuinely glad to see me. And I was just as glad to find her wearing that red apron for a living. After visiting for a few minutes, I realized something I'd never noticed before. Beneath her hardshell exterior was a regular lady, working from nine to five for pennies. She was doing the best she could with her life. Just like me.

Before I left, she asked me what kind of work I did.

At the time, I worked in construction.

SEAN DIETRICH

Sean Dietrich is a writer, humorist, and novelist, known for his commentary on life in the American South. His humor and short fiction appear in various publications throughout the Southeast, including South Magazine, *the* Tallahassee Democrat, Wired Magazine, Food Network Blog, Outdoors Magazine, *and he is a member of the NWU. His first short story was published during childhood, in a hometown journal newspaper. Since then, he's pursued his literary interests authoring four novels, writing humor, and short stories.*

An avid sailor and fisherman, when he's not writing, he spends much of his time aboard his sailboat (The S.S. Squirrel), *riding the Gulf of Mexico trying not to die, along with his coonhound, Ellie Mae.*

FOR MORE STORIES, OR TO CONTACT SEAN, VISIT:
WWW.SEANDIETRICH.COM

Made in the USA
Coppell, TX
22 January 2024